Englischunterricht bis Klasse 4

Name ______________________ Klasse ____________

1 Hast du in den Klassen 1 bis 4 schon Englisch gelernt?

☐ nein ☐ ja, und zwar
☐ seit der 1. Klasse
☐ seit der 3. Klasse

☐ eine Stunde in der Woche
☐ zwei / ☐ drei Stunden in der Woche
☐ ______________________

2 Habt ihr im Englischunterricht meistens englisch miteinander gesprochen?

☐ nein ☐ ja

3 Kreuze an, was du schon auf Englisch sagen kannst:

☐ guten Tag / ☐ auf Wiedersehen
☐ bitte / ☐ danke
☐ das Alphabet
☐ die Zahlen von 1–10 / ☐ von ____ – ____
☐ wie viel etwas kostet
☐ wie spät es ist
☐ die Wochentage / ☐ die Monatsnamen

☐ wie du heißt
☐ wie es dir geht
☐ wo du wohnst
☐ wie alt du bist
☐ wann dein Geburtstag ist
☐ ob du Geschwister hast
☐ was du magst/nicht magst

4a Habt ihr englische Geschichten von CDs oder Cassetten gehört? ☐ oft ☐ selten/nie

b An welche Geschichten kannst du dich erinnern, weil sie dir besonders gefallen haben?

____

5 Kreuze die Themen und Feste an, über die ihr im Englischunterricht gesprochen habt:

☐ Farben
☐ Essen
☐ Spiele und Hobbys
☐ Einkaufen
☐ dein Körper

☐ Schulsachen
☐ Haus/Wohnung
☐ Familie
☐ Tiere
☐ Kleidung

☐ Christmas
☐ Halloween
☐ Easter
☐ Valentine's Day

Außerdem:

____

6 Hast du auch außerhalb des Unterrichts Englisch gelernt?

☐ mit deinen Eltern ☐ am Computer ☐ mit anderen Kindern

7 Was hast du beim Englischlernen besonders gern gemacht?

☐ Geschichten gehört
☐ Rätsel gelöst
☐ Lieder gesungen

☐ Gedichte/Reime aufgesagt
☐ Wörter geschrieben
☐ Spiele gespielt
☐ Sketche/Dialoge gespielt

Außerdem:

____

8a Hast du bereits ein Portfolio angelegt? ☐ nein ☐ ja

b Wenn ja, was hat dir daran am meisten Spaß gemacht?

____

1 Hello, Polly! ▸ p. 8

a) *Read and write.*

Hello. My name is Polly. Pretty Polly!
I'm 5 years old. I'm from Bristol.
My favourite colour is red. Yes, red, red.

1 What's your name?
2 How old are you?
3 Where are you from?
4 What's your favourite colour?

YOU

1 My name ______________________ ______________________.

2 I'm ______________ ______________ old.

3 I ________ from ______________________.

4 My ______________________ is ______________________.

b) *Write questions.*

1 name/What's/your ? ______________________

2 you/How/old/are ? ______________________

3 you/Where/from/are ? ______________________

0301
0302
4 your/colour/What's/favourite? ______________________

2 New names ▸ p. 8

a) Write.

1 This is Polly.
2 This ______.
3 ______

4 ______
5 ______

b) Match and write.

She's 11 years old. | They're twins. | She's new in Bristol. | She's 11 years old. | They're from Bristol. | He's from Bristol. | They're 12 years old. | She's from Bristol. | He's 11 years old.

1 Write about Ananda. ______
2 Write about Jack. ______
3 Write about Dan and Jo. ______
______
4 Write about Sophie. ______

Now you

Write about a boy and a girl in your class.

(Name) ______. He's ______.

0402 (Name) ______. She's ______.

3 WORDS What can you see? ▸ p. 9

a) *Write the correct numbers in the box.*

(1) boat	( ) kite	( ) water	( ) trees	( ) skateboard
( ) football	( ) house	( ) boy	( ) girls	( ) boys

b) *Write the words.*

I can see a b o a t and w _ _ _ _ and two g _ _ _ _

with a _ _ _ _ .

I can see twc _ _ _ _ with a _ _ _ _ _ _ _ _ and a _ _ _

with a red _ _ _ _ _ _ _ _ _ _ .

I can see a _ _ _ _ _ and three _ _ _ _ _ too.

c) *Write correct words.*

0503
0504

t b a o ________ b l f o t o l a ________

a t r e w ________ b s o a t r d k e a ________

4 WORDS A word kite ▸ pp. 10–11

Find and write.

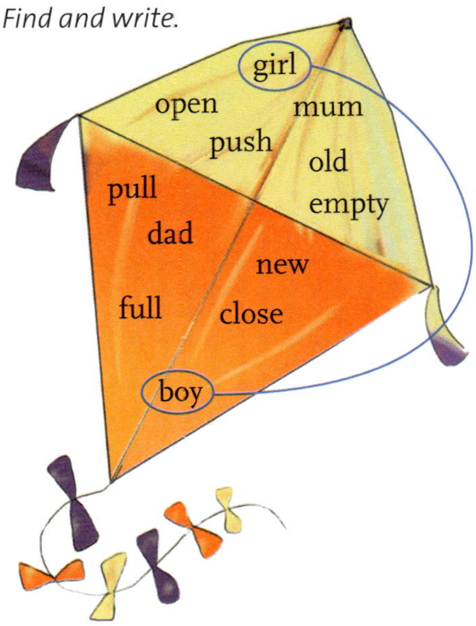

girl	–	boy
	–	
	–	
	–	
	–	
	–	

5 WORDS Dan's school shopping list ▸ p. 12

a) *Match and write.*

shopping		book
pencil		list
school		case
exercise		bag
glue		stick
pencil		tip
felt		sharpener

! Two words.

shopping list

______

______

______

______

______

______

b) *Draw and write the names of four things from your school bag.*

1	2	3	4	5
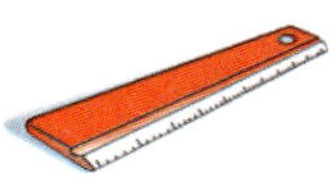				
ruler				

0605

6 WORDS Colour words ▸ p. 13

Find and colour the colour words.

7 Prunella's plates ▸ p. 13

What colours are Prunella's plates? Write the colours.

blue

Rhyme time*

* *Zeit für einen Reim*

One plate, two plates,
Three plates, four.
Five plates, six plates,
Two plates more[1].
Seven plates and one
Are eight.
Crash! Bang! Wallop!
My favourite plate ...
Aaaaw!

Now you

What's your favourite colour? It's ______________________.

What colour is your school bag? ______________________

What colour is your pencil case? ______________________

0707 What colour is your glue stick? ______________________

8 What day is it? ▸ p. 14

Write the day. Look at the pictures and Jo's diary[2].

It's Monday.

M – badminton
T – pizza with Dad
W – football
T – shopping with Dad (new football?)
F – party
S – help Dad in house
S – new DVDs!!

[1] more [mɔː] *mehr* [2] diary ['daɪəri] *Terminkalender*

9 Find the house numbers ▸ p. 15

a) *Match six house numbers to the speech bubbles. Write the correct numbers from the box.*

My house number is thirteen. ____
Ananda

I live at number seventeen. ____

Sophie

We live at number seven. ____

Dan and Jo

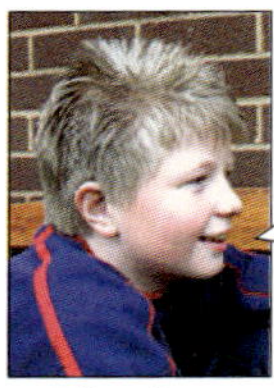
I live at number forty-two. ____
Florian

We live at number twenty-four. ____
Tim and Becky

My house number is twenty-eight. ____

Jack

b) *Now write the red house numbers in words.*

0809

____

10 Who am I? ▸ p. 15

a) *Read the secret code[1] and write the letters in the speech bubble.*

37	36	35	34	33	32	31	30	29	28	27	26	25	24	23	22	21	20	19	18	17	16	15	14	13	12
A	B	C	D	E	F	G	H	I	J	K	L	M	N	O	P	Q	R	S	T	U	V	W	X	Y	Z

__ __   __ __ __ __   __ __   __ __ __ __ __ __ __ __.
__ __ __ __, __   __ __ __ __   __ __ __ __?

Start here:
twenty-five thirteen twenty-four thirty-seven twenty-five thirty-three
twenty-nine nineteen thirty-six thirty-seven twenty twenty-four thirty-seven thirty-six
thirty-seven nineteen fifteen thirty thirty-seven eighteen nineteen thirteen
twenty-three seventeen twenty twenty-four thirty-seven twenty-five thirty-three

b) *Write your answer in code. Write the numbers in words.*

My name is very nice.

____

____

____

[1] secret code [siːkrət ˈkəʊd] *Geheimcode*

11 What's the time? ▸ pp. 16–17

Draw the time on the clocks.

It's seven o'clock. | It's quarter to five. | It's half past ten. | It's quarter past four.

It's five twenty-five. | It's four thirty-six. | It's twelve o two.

12 Prunella's clocks ▸ pp. 16–17

Look at Prunella's clocks. Write the times.

1 It's ______________________.

2 ______________________

3 ______________________

4 ______________________

5 ______________________

6 ______________________

0912 *One clock is right. Which clock is it?* – Clock number ___ ___ ___ ___ is right.

Now you

What's the time now? It's ______________________.

13 WORDS S-words ▸ p. 17

Read and write.

1 Can you sing a ...?
2 The Kapoors live in a flat over a ...
3 *Dilip*: Ananda is my ...
4 The ... holidays are great.
5 ... is the last day of the week.
6 Day six of the week is ...
7 I can see a boy with a red ...

1 s o n g
2 s _ _ _
3 _ _ _ _ _ _
4 _ _ _ _ _ _
5 _ _ _ _ _ _
6 _ _ _ _ _ _ _ _
7 _ _ _ _ _ _ _ _ _ _

0913
0914

Unit 1 New school, new friends

1 WORDS What's in the picture? (there is/are) ▸ p. 18–19

a) *Write the names of the things.*

1 ___ ___ ___ ___ ___ ___ [ ] ___ ___
6 [ ] ___ ___ ___ ___ ___ ___ s
8 ___ ___ ___ ___ [ ] ___ ___ ___ ___ s
7 [ ] ___ ___ ___ ___ s
4 ___ [ ] ___ ___ ___ ___ ___ ___ ___ ___ ___
2 ___ ___ ___ ___ ___ ___ ___ ___ [ ] ___
9 ___ ___ [ ] ___ s
3 ___ ___ ___ ___ ___ [ ] ___ ___ ___ ___ ___
5 ___ ___ ___ ___ [ ]

b) *Make a new word with the letters from the blue boxes in a). What is it? Write it in the speech bubble.*

c) *Look at the picture again. What is there? Write sentences with* **there is** *or* **there are**.

1 There's a school bag.
2
3
4
5
6 There are two felt tips.
7
8
9

1000
1001

2 PRONUNCIATION *a* or *an* ▸ p. 19 2

Say the words with a or an and write them in the correct list.
Then listen to the CD and check your lists.

nice day English book
apple yellow pen
newspaper old picture
empty room ruler
orange bag uniform
exercise new word

1102

a	an
a nice day	an English book

3 WORDS Day one ▸ p. 20

Write words from the boxes.

students year nervous twins first welcome Room

w e l c o m e to the new school!

It's day one of the new school _ _ _ _ .

The new _ _ _ _ _ _ _ _ are at school.

Lessons are in _ _ _ _ 14.

Before lessons the _ _ _ _ _ , Dan and Jo, are _ _ _ _ _ _ _ .

Dan: You go _ _ _ _ _ , Jo. – *Jo:* No, you.

Rhyme time

School bag,
Pencil case,
Glue stick too.
First day of school for me,
What about you?

4 *He, she, it, ...* (Personal pronouns) ▸ p. 20 • GF 1 (p. 131)

Match and colour.

HE SHE IT THEY

mum and dad	brother	girl	Ananda	Sophie
classroom	Dan and Jo	Jo	Mr Shaw	Mrs Kapoor
Prunella	colour	twins	dad	students
school	pen	name	books	Jack

1104

5 Hello! (Personal pronouns) ▸ p. 20 • GF 1 (p. 131)

Write I, you, he, she, it, we or they.

Jo Hello. My name is Jo, and this is my brother Dan. *We*’re twins.

Florian Hi. My name is Florian.

Dan Florian? ______’s a German[1] name, right? Is your dad German?

Florian Yes, ______’s from Essen.

Dan Is your mum German too?

Florian No, ______’s English. ______’s from Bristol.
______’re very happy in Bristol. ______’s a nice place.

Sophie Hello. ______’m Sophie. Oh, ______’re new in Bristol too.

Florian Hi, Sophie. ______’m Florian. That’s Dan and that’s Jo. ______’ re twins.

Teacher Ah, hello. ______’re the new students. Well, this is Room 14.
______’s a nice room. Let’s go.

6 I’m Dan (be: positive statements) ▸ p. 20 • GF 1, 2 (pp. 131–132)

Complete with short forms: I’m, you’re, he’s, she’s, it’s, we’re, you’re, they’re.

1206

[1] German ['dʒɜːmən] *deutsch*

7 What's wrong? (be: positive and negative statements)

▸ p. 21 • GF 2 (p. 132)

Correct the sentences. Write short forms.

1 Toby is ten years old.

He isn't ten years old. He's eight years old.

2 It's half past eight.

____

3 Jack and Ananda are at the B&B.

____

4 Polly is fifty years old.

____

5 'Dan, you're from London, right?'

Wrong. ______________________________

8 Questions and answers (be)

▸ p. 21 • GF 2 (p. 132)

Write questions and short answers.

1 Prunella/a/Is/poltergeist ?

Is Prunella a poltergeist? | *Yes, she is.*

2 Mr Kapoor/from Uganda/Is ?

______________________________ | ______________

3 a parrot/Sheeba/Is ?

______________________________ | ______________

4 Jack/twelve/and/Ananda/Are ?

1308

______________________________ | ______________

9 WORDS A puzzle ▸ p. 22

Write the words in the puzzle, then find the word in the pink boxes.

1 Please ... me your names.
2 Can you ... your name, please?
3 *Mr Kingsley:* It isn't a joke. Please, don't ...
4 *Ananda:* I can't play football, but I can play ...
5 And ... are you? What's your name?
6 Write your name on the board, ...
7 You're in ... 7PK.

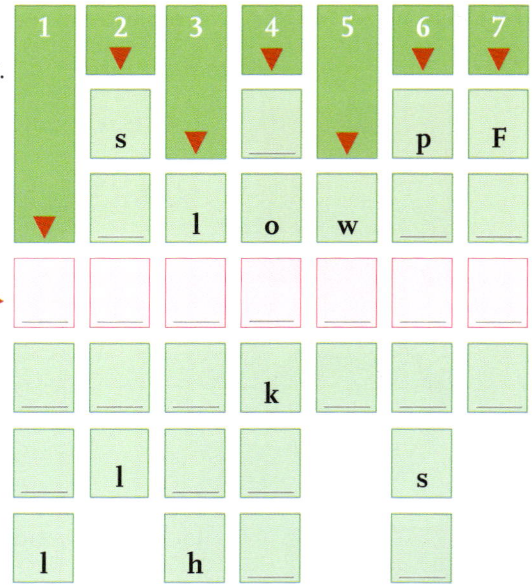

▶ Who is your English _ _ _ _ _ _ _ ?

My ______________________________

______________________________.

10 Can you do this? (can/can't) ▸ p. 22 • GF 3 (p. 133)

Write sentences with ***can*** *or* ***can't***.

1  *I can do this.*

2  ______________________________

3  ______________________________

4  ______________________________

11 What can they do? (can/can't) ▸ p. 22 • GF 3 (p. 133)

Can *or* ***can't****? Write sentences.*

He • She • They	can can't	play hockey • see Polly • help in the shop • talk • *sing* • see Prunella

1 

She can't sing.

2 

____

3 

____

4 

____

5 

____

6 

____

1411

12 Dos and Don'ts (Imperatives) ▸ p. 23 • GF 4 (p. 134)

Complete the sentences.

be (2x) • sing • stop • talk • drop • eat • play

1

Mrs Hanson: Polly, be ________ quiet, please! Don't talk! ________

2

Jack: Polly, ________ my apple! It's for school.

3

Jack: Please ________ ________ my felt tips, Polly.

4

Jack: Polly! ________ with my mobile phone!

1512

5

Jack: Ouch!! ________ that, Polly. ________ nice.

6

Mr Hanson: Polly! It's six o'clock on Sunday morning. Please ________ now!

13 WORDS School subjects ▸ p. 23

Find the school subjects in the '?'. Write the subjects under the correct pictures.

Science ________

____

____

____

____

____

____

____

____

____

____

____

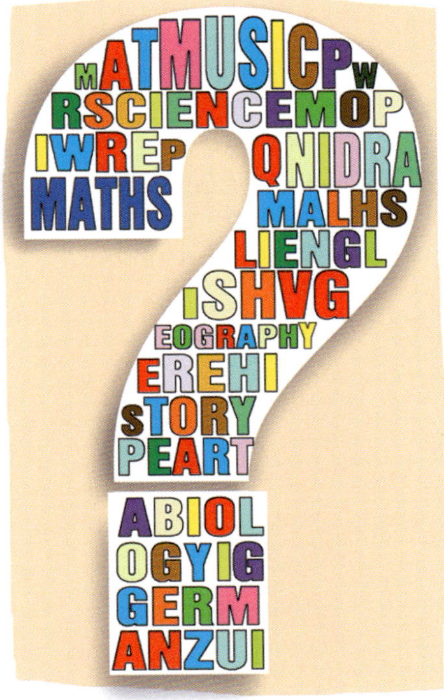

Now you

Look at your timetable.

1 What's lesson 1 on Monday?

It's ______________________.

2 What's lesson 2 on Wednesday?

____

3 What's after the first break on Tuesday?

____

4 What's the last lesson on Friday?

____

5 What's your favourite subject?

____

14 WORDS Where are the school words?

▸ p. 23

a) *Find and write the school words.*

p	b	r	e	a	k	b	S	l
s	o	j	k	y	s	o	c	e
M	a	t	h	s	u	o	i	s
y	r	w	q	p	b	k	e	s
v	d	s	f	e	j	x	n	o
m	p	u	h	l	e	d	c	n
F	o	r	m	l	c	s	e	s
M	u	s	i	c	t	w	m	q
t	i	m	e	t	a	b	l	e
j	p	t	e	a	c	h	e	r

1614

Look! Look!
I can see **break**. And **board**. Yes, yes! **Board**!

▶	▼
break	board

b) *Fill in words from a).*

1 We can play football in the b r e a k.

2 Can you _ _ _ _ _ 'favourite', please?

3 Are you in _ _ _ _ 7PK?

4 Jo, write 'Science' on the _ _ _ _ _, please.

5 English _ _ _ _ _ _ _ are great.

6 My favourite _ _ _ _ _ _ _ is English.

7 Is PE on Monday? – Look at the _ _ _ _ _ _ _ _ _.

Just for fun*

* Nur zum Spaß

A: 'Poltergeist' is a long word. Can you spell it, please?
B: Yes, I can. P-O-L ...
A: Wrong. It's I-T!

15 WORDS Lists ▸ p. 23

Write the words in three lists.

throw	write	nervous	laugh	quiet	listen	lunch
student	wrong	meet	marmalade	white	timetable	think
	breakfast	clever	great	come		

VERBS

throw,

ADJECTIVES

nervous, quiet,

NOUNS

lunch,

1715

16 STUDY SKILLS Wörter lernen ▸ p. 23 • SF 1 (pp. 122–123)

a) *Schau dir in deinem Buch das Vocabulary zu Unit 1 auf den Seiten 156 bis 160 gut an. Es ist viel mehr als eine Wortliste. Welche Informationen findest du dort?*

Überlege gut und mach ein Häkchen (✓) in die entsprechenden Kästchen:

Im Vocabulary finde ich ...

- ..., wie ich ein Wort aussprechen muss. ☐
- ..., wie ich ein Wort betonen muss. ☐
- ... Grammatikregeln. ☐
- ... Paare von Gegensätzen. ☐
- ..., wie ich Aufsätze schreiben kann. ☐
- ... Hinweise auf Fehlerquellen. ☐

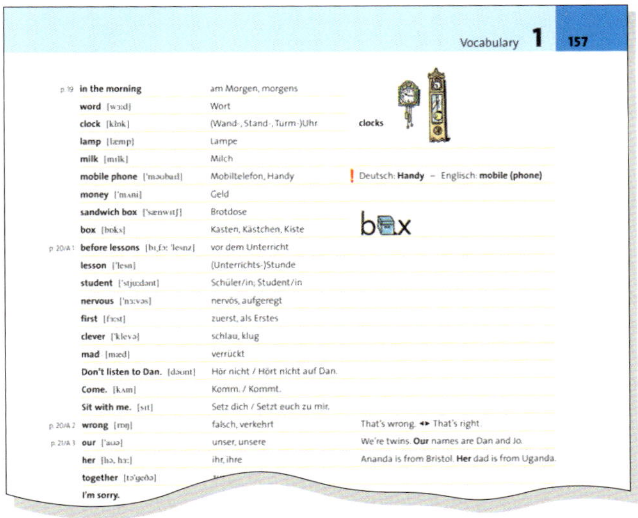
Vocabulary 1 157

p. 19	**in the morning**	am Morgen, morgens	
	word [wɜːd]	Wort	
	clock [klɒk]	(Wand-, Stand-, Turm-)Uhr	clocks
	lamp [læmp]	Lampe	
	milk [mɪlk]	Milch	
	mobile phone [ˈməʊbaɪl]	Mobiltelefon, Handy	! Deutsch: **Handy** – Englisch: **mobile (phone)**
	money [ˈmʌni]	Geld	
	sandwich box [ˈsænwɪtʃ]	Brotdose	
	box [bɒks]	Kasten, Kästchen, Kiste	box
p. 20/A 1	**before lessons** [bɪˌfɔː ˈlesnz]	vor dem Unterricht	
	lesson [ˈlesn]	(Unterrichts-)Stunde	
	student [ˈstjuːdənt]	Schüler/in; Student/in	
	nervous [ˈnɜːvəs]	nervös, aufgeregt	
	first [fɜːst]	zuerst, als Erstes	
	clever [ˈklevə]	schlau, klug	
	mad [mæd]	verrückt	
	Don't listen to Dan. [dəʊnt]	Hör nicht / Hört nicht auf Dan.	
	Come. [kʌm]	Komm. / Kommt.	
	Sit with me. [sɪt]	Setz dich / Setzt euch zu mir.	
p. 20/A 2	**wrong** [rɒŋ]	falsch, verkehrt	That's wrong. ◂▸ That's right.
p. 21/A 3	**our** [ˈaʊə]	unser, unsere	We're twins. **Our** names are Dan and Jo.
	her [hə, hɜː]	ihr, ihre	Ananda is from Bristol. **Her** dad is from Uganda.
	together [təˈgeðə]		
	I'm sorry.		

● ***b)*** *Suche im Vocabulary auf der Seite 157 ...*

1 *... ein englisches Wort, das dem deutschen Wort ähnelt, aber anders betont wird:*

___

2 *... zwei englische Wörter, die Gegensätze sind:*

___

3 *... einen Hinweis auf eine Besonderheit, bei der man leicht einen Fehler machen kann (!):*

___

17 WORDS New words ▸ p. 23

Make new words from the ***green*** *words. Find eight or more words.*

teacher: cat, eat, ______________________

____

badminton: to, ______________________

____

timetable: ______________________

____

18 Who has got what? (have got/has got) ▸ p. 24 • GF 5 (pp. 134–135)

a) *Four boys have got a skateboard, a kite, a football and a dog. Who is who? Write the names.*
Ed's favourite number is thirteen. Michael and Ed haven't got a dog.
Tony hasn't got a kite.

______________ ______________ ______________ ______________

b) *Who has got a skateboard, a kite, a football or a dog? Complete the sentences with* ***has got****.*

Ed has got a ______________________. Alexander ______________________.

Michael ______________________. Tony ______________________.

c) *Now write sentences with* ***hasn't got****.*

Ed hasn't got a skateboard, a kite or a ______________________.

Alexander ______________________ or ______________________.

Michael ______________________ or ______________________.

Tony ______________________ or ______________________.

19 What have they got? (have got/has got)

▸ p. 24 • GF 5 (pp. 134–135)

Complete with: **have got**, **has got** (✓), **haven't got**, **hasn't got** (✗)

Ananda	✓	✓	✓	✗
Dan	✗	✓	✓	✓
Jo	✗	✗	✓	✓

Ananda *has got* a mobile phone. She *hasn't got* a pet, but she ______ lots of books.

Dan and Jo ______ pets, but they ______ an MP3 player.

Jo ______ lots of books, but he ______ a mobile phone. Ananda and Dan

1919 ______ lots of books. One student ______ an MP3 player. Who is it?

20 Questions and answers (have got/has got)

▸ p. 24 • GF 5 (pp. 134–135)

Write questions with **have got**. *Then write short answers:* **Yes, she has.** /... / **No, they haven't.** /...

1 Sophie/a sister?

Q: *Has Sophie got a sister?* A: *Yes, she has.*

2 Ananda/a brother?

Q: ______ A: ______

3 Sophie/a parrot?

Q: ______ A: ______

4 the Hansons/a B&B?

Q: ______ A: ______

5 Dan and Jo/a dog?

Q: ______ A: ______

Now you

Write short answers.

1 Have you got a sister? ______

2 Has your friend got a brother? ______

3 Have you got a pet? ______

21 WORDS Find the words ▸ p. 24

Match and colour. Then write correct words.

cise | emp | ough | ence | teach | time | table | ea | id | Sci | real | ty | ing | day | mor | er | exer | en | ly | sic | Geog | ter | pos | Tues | Mu | raphy | ning | bor

timetable

exercise

22 About you ▸ p. 33

*First read about Jo. Then write about you. You can change the **green** words.*

My name is Jo. I'm twelve years old and I'm from Bristol. I'm a student at Cotham School. My English teacher is Mr Kingsley. My favourite subject is PE. I can play basketball, but I can't play tennis. I've got a brother. I haven't got a sister, but I've got lots of nice friends.

My name is

2022
2023

23 READING Meet the Baxters ▸ p. 33

a) *Read about Tim, Becky and Barnabas.*

Hello, I'm Tim Baxter. I'm eleven years old and I'm in Form 7SB. School is OK.
My favourite subject is Science. I can't spell or do French, but I can do Maths and play badminton. I can climb trees too.
My favourite day is Saturday. I've got lots of comics in my room – in my school bag too.
I've got a sister, Becky – well, Rebecca really, and a great pet, Barnabas.

Hi, I'm Becky. Tennis is great. I can play tennis, but I can't do tricks or climb trees.
I've got lots of posters in my room. Tim is my little brother. He's nice, clever too.
Oh, I'm thirteen and I'm in Form 8JW. My favourite subject is Art. My favourite day is Saturday.

Hello. My name is Barnabas – not 'Barney', please. Tim is my friend. I'm his pet. Tim is eleven. Me too. Becky is nice, but Tim is very nice.
Well, I can ..., I can ... sit on the skateboard. I can't play badminton, but I can play CDs.
My favourite show is 'Super Cat'. Cats are great. But parrots aren't great. Polly is not my friend. Oh, and my favourite day is – ermm – Sunday!

● ***b)*** *What's right? Check the text and find out.*

	Tim	Becky	Barnabas
How old?	11/12/10	11/12/13	9/10/11
Form	7SB/8JW/7PK	8JW/7SB/7PK	–
Can ...	spell/do Maths/ do French	do tricks/play tennis/ climb trees	sit on the skateboard/ play badminton
Favourite day	Saturday/Friday/Sunday	Monday/Sunday/Saturday	Saturday/Sunday
Favourite subject	RE/Science/French	Art/English/RE	–
Has got ...	lots of comics/ lots of books	lots of posters/ lots of photos	–

● ***c)*** *Right or wrong? Correct the wrong sentences.*

1 Tim can play badminton. Right.

2 Barnabas is ten years old. Wrong. He's eleven years old.

3 Tim has got lots of football posters. ______

4 Becky can do tricks. ______

5 Becky is fourteen. ______

6 Barnabas can play CDs. ______

24 Months of the year ▸ p. 34

You can write eight months of the year with the letters. Which months are they?

A B C D E F H J L M N O R T U Y

____

2224 ______________________________

25 Find the month ▸ p. 34

Write down the letters from the boxes. When is Prunella's birthday? One month is correct.

My first is in red. F or D

My second is in blue. ____ or ____

My third is in green. ____ or ____

My fourth is in brown. ____ or ____

My fifth is in purple. ____ or ____

My sixth is in yellow. ____ or ____

My seventh is in pink. ____ or ____

My eighth is in white. ____ or ____

26 Prunella's birthday calendar ▸ p. 34

Write the dates of the birthdays.

Emily – 01. 06.	Emily's birthday is on 1st June.
Toby – 03. 07.	Toby's birthday ______________________.
Hannah – 22. 10.	Hannah's birthday ______________________.
Sophie – 26. 03.	Sophie's birthday ______________________.
Sheeba – 21. 05.	Sheeba's birthday ______________________.

Now you

When's your birthday? My ______________________.

When's your friend's birthday? My friend's ______________________.

1 What can you see in the classroom?

1 ____________ 5 ____________

2 ____________ 6 ____________

3 ____________ 7 ____________

4 ____________ 8 ____________

2 Complete.

1 

2 

3 

Barnabas ________ a parrot.
He ____________ a cat.

'I ______ a very nice pet.
I ___________ a mad cat!'

They ___________ classmates.
They _____ brother and sister.

3 Write what they *have got* and what they *haven't got*.

1 The Hansons ____________________ a B&B. It ________________________ five rooms.

2 The Kapoors ___________________________ a house. They ____________________ a flat and a shop.

3 Ananda ____________________ a brother, but she ___________________________ a pet.

20 points

Now you

First read about a new friend. Then write to the new friend about you.

Hi!

I'm your new friend from Australia. My name is Leo and I'm 12 years old. I've got a sister, Kim. She's 14. I can play tennis and football too.
My favourite subject is Science. I like History too. I've got lots of nice friends.
What about you?
Please write!

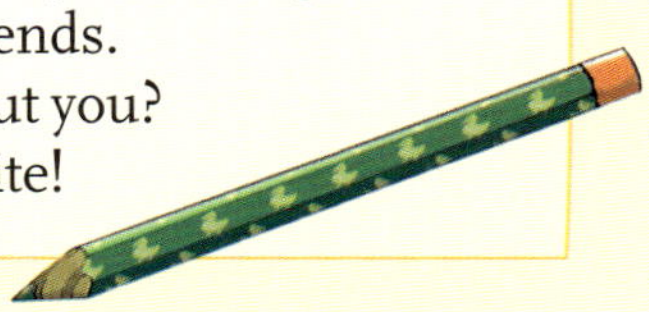

Hi!

I'm your new friend from Germany. My name is ____________________

____

____

____

____

____

____

2304
2305

Unit 2 A weekend at home

1 WORDS Tim's room ▸ p. 36

○ ***a)** Label the things in the pictures.*

bed • chair • clock • desk • lamp • photos • shelf • wardrobe • window

① ____________ ② ____________

③ ____________ ④ ____________ ⑤ ____________ ⑥ ____________

⑦ ____________ ⑧ ____________ ⑨ ____________

***b)** Now read about Tim's room. Is it picture 1 or picture 2?*

My room is white – oh, and orange, my favourite colour. You can see houses and the park from my window. There's a bed, a desk and a chair and there's a big wardrobe. I can throw all my things in there. There's a big poster and a photo of Barnabas. There's a shelf for books, CDs and school things and there's a lamp on my desk. I've got a computer and lots of great games.
I'm happy with my room. It's really nice.

2400
2401 Tim's room is ____________________ .

2 REVISION *be* ▸ p. 36 • GF 2 (p. 132)

Look at exercise **1** *again. Write short answers:* ***Yes, it is.*** / ***No, …***

Is Tim's room white and orange? ____________________

Is his chair blue? ____________________

Is Barnabas in Tim's photos? ____________________

Are all Tim's CDs on his shelf? ____________________

Rhyme time

My room isn't big,
My things aren't new,
My bed is old,
My wardrobe too.
My desk is red,
My lamp is blue.
I ♥ my room,
What about you?

Now you

Write about your room. Use ideas from exercise **1**: ***My room is … There's a … There are …***

____

____

____

____

3 WORDS Pets ► p. 37

Label the pets.

budgie • cat • dog • fish • guinea pig • hamster • horse • mouse • rabbit • tortoise • parrot

1  ____________

2  ____________

3  ____________

4  ____________

5  ____________

6  ____________

7  ____________

8  ____________

9  ____________

10  ____________

11  ____________

2503

4 REVISION Where the Bristol pets live (have got/has got) ► p. 37 • GF 5a (p. 134)

a) *What is it? Label the pictures.*

1  ____________

2  ____________

3  ____________

Rhyme time

A budgie, a guinea pig,
A tortoise too.
I've got lots of pets,
What about you?

b) *What have the pets got? Write sentences.*

Polly Bill and Ben Hip and Hop Sheeba Harry	have got has got	a hutch a cage a basket	... bedroom. ... living room. ... kitchen. ... garden.

Polly *has got a cage in the living room.*

Bill and Ben ____________________________________.

Hip and Hop ____________________________________.

____

____

5 PRONUNCIATION Plurals

▸ p. 38 • GF 6 (p. 135) 3

Listen to the words. Colour the last letters ***red***, ***blue*** *or* ***green***.

Look:

[-s]	[-z]	[-ɪz]
cats	girls	houses

classes

kites pets hands days

windows baskets flats pages jokes

tortoises horses lessons numbers

6 A day in the life of … (Simple present: positive statements)

▸ p. 38 • GF 7a (p. 136)

a) *Complete with words from the box.*

get up (2x) • help • meet • go • make • have • read • talk • think • work

Ananda: Mum, this is my essay for Mr Kingsley. It's about a day in my life. Listen, please, and tell me what you think ____.

I ________ at 7.30 every morning. My mum and dad ________ at 6.30. They ________ in our shop. We ________ breakfast together at 7.45. I ________ tea and toast for all the family. My mum and dad ________ the newspapers. My brother Dilip and I ________ about school and friends. Every morning we ________ in the shop and then we ________ to school. Before lessons I ________ my friends. Then I …

Oh, no, no, no! This essay is boring! I can't read this at school …

b) *What's wrong with this essay? Write the sentences again with the* ***green*** *words in the right place.*

I go to bed at 7.30 in the morning. First, I have lunch. Then I wash my face and clean my teeth in the kitchen with my mum. At school we play football in Room 14. At 12.40 we all have breakfast at school. After school we have lessons in the park.
I get up at 9.30 in the evening.

I get up at 7.30 in the morning.

____

____

____

____

____

____

____

2606

7 STUDY SKILLS Mindmaps

▸ p. 38 • SF 3 (p. 125)

Make a mind map about ***My Saturday*** *in your exercise book.*
You can use these ideas:

write e-mails · read in bed · get up late · in the evening · go to bed at … · *in the morning* · *in the afternoon* · have breakfast · play football · meet my friends · go to the shops · listen to CDs · play with my pet · have lunch · clean my teeth · go to the park · wash my face

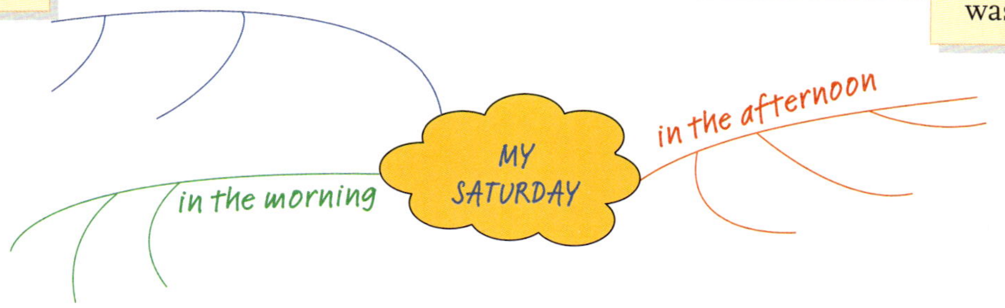

2707
2708

8 -s, -es or -ies? (Simple present: 3rd person singular)

▸ p. 39 • GF 7b (p. 137)

Write the verbs in the correct lists.

clean • go • hurry • listen • push • sleep • try • eat • wash • watch

-s: cleans, ____________________

-es: goes, ____________________

-ies: hurries, ____________________

9 Becky's weekends (Simple present: 3rd person singular)

▸ p. 39 • GF 7b (p. 137)

Write sentences about Becky's weekends.

1 

get up – 9 o'clock

2 
go to the shops

3 
play tennis – park

4 
watch TV – her family

5 
help mum – kitchen

1 On Saturdays she gets up at 9 o'clock.

2 Before lunch she ____________________.

3 In the afternoon ____________________.

4 In the evening ____________________.

2709 5 On Sunday ____________________.

10 Sundays (Simple present: positive statements)

▸ p. 39 • GF 7a–b (pp. 136–137)

Complete Sophie's text.

First we *have* (have) breakfast together in the kitchen. Mum *makes* (make) tea and toast.

Dad ______ (eat) lots of marmalade. Toby ______ (like) cornflakes.

After breakfast we ______ (go) to the park with Sheeba. Emily ______ (go) too.

Then we ______ (help) Mum with lunch. Well, Dad ______ (watch) TV, or he ______ (read) his newspapers. After lunch Hannah and Sheeba ______ (sleep).

Emily ______ (talk) to all her friends on her mobile phone. In the evenings we ______ (listen) to music or we ______ (watch) TV. I really ______ (like) Sundays.

2810

● Now you

Write three sentences about your Sundays. Use ideas from Sophie's text and: **First ... After that ... Then...**

We get up late on Sundays. First

______

______

○ 11 WORDS Find the right word

▸ p. 40

Match two fish, colour the fish, then write one new word.

newspaper,

______

12 Right or wrong? (Simple present: negative statements) ► p. 40 • GF 7c (p. 137)

Mark the sentences right (√) or wrong (x).
Write sentences with ***don't*** *for the wrong sentences.*

1 All pets need water. ✓
2 Horses live in hutches. X Horses don't live in hutches.
3 Horses eat apples. ______
4 Hamsters like marmalade. ______
5 Rabbits eat fish. ______
6 Dogs go to school. ______
7 Cats drink tea. ______
2912 8 Parrots need food. ______

13 REVISION Words ► p. 40

Which words go together? Match and write.

tell jokes
______
______
______
______
______
______
______

14 What Prunella does (Simple present: positive and negative statements) ▸ p. 40 • GF 7 (pp. 136–137)

Write about Prunella. Write about what she does (✓) and what she doesn't do (✗).

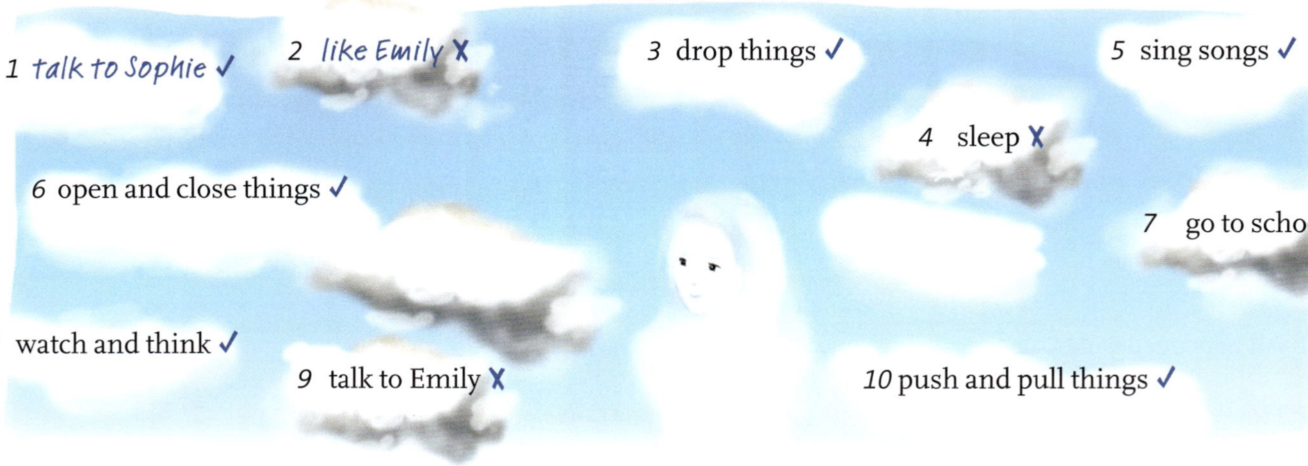

1) She talks to Sophie. 2) She doesn't like Emily.

____

____

____

____

15 WORDS Family words ▸ p. 41

Put the family words from the box in the right list. Which words go together?

aunt • brother • daughter • father • grandma • grandpa • mother • sister • son • uncle

mother	father

Now you

Write about your family. Have you got brothers or sisters? Have you got grandparents, aunts, uncles and cousins?

I've got a ____

____

____

16 Who are they? (Possessive form)

▸ p. 41 • GF 9 (p. 138)

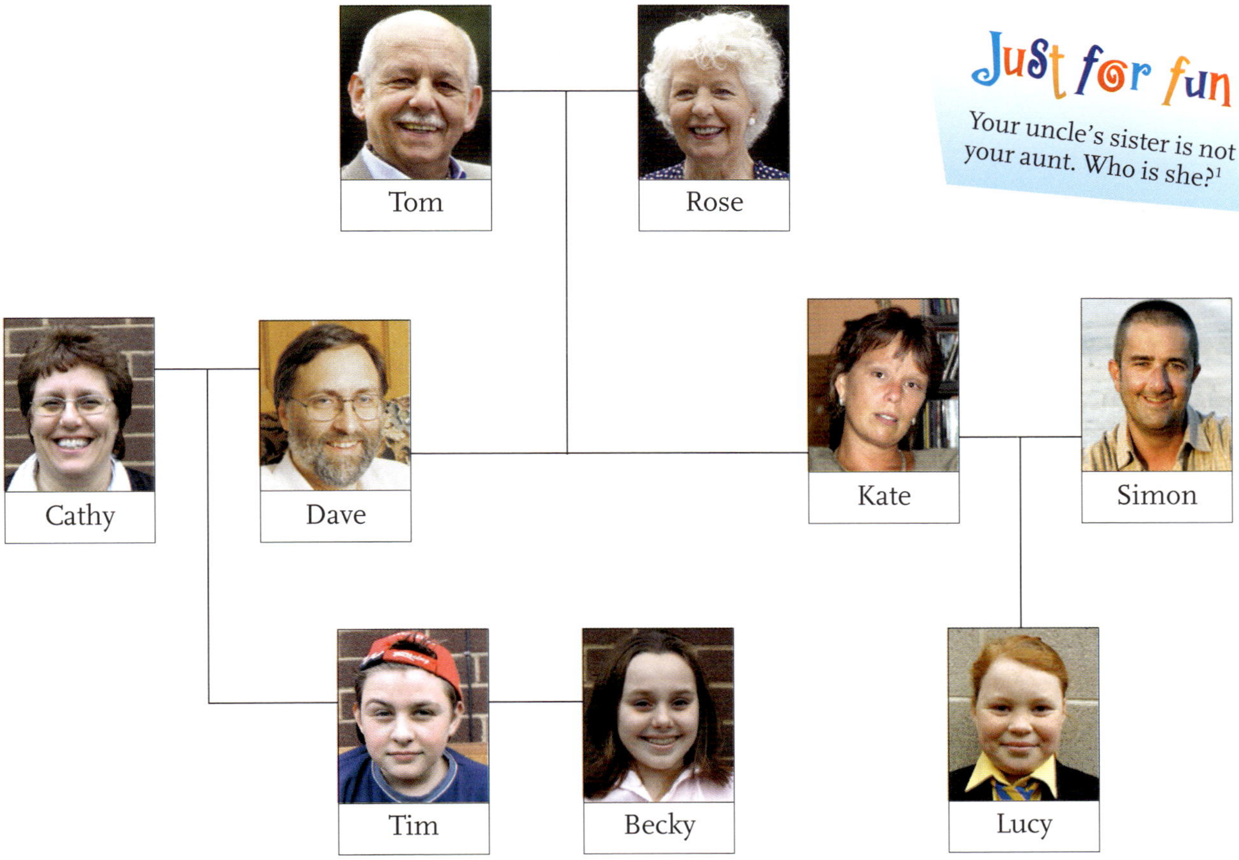

Just for fun

Your uncle's sister is not your aunt. Who is she?[1]

a) *Look at the Baxters' family tree. Who's who? Is it a), b) or c)? Sometimes two are correct.*

1 Tom is a) Simon's brother. b) Dave's uncle. c) Lucy's grandfather. (circled)

2 Tim is a) Becky's cousin. b) Dave and Cathy's son. c) Lucy's brother.

3 Lucy is a) Tim and Becky's cousin. b) Cathy's aunt. c) Kate and Simon's daughter.

4 Cathy is a) Lucy's aunt. b) Tim and Becky's mother. c) Lucy's mother.

5 Rose is a) Tom's daughter. b) Simon's aunt. c) Dave and Kate's mother.

● ***b)*** *Now complete what Tim says about his family. Use 's or s'.*

Tim: This is the Baxters' family tree. Look. I'm Tim and my sister's name is Becky. My ________ name is Kate and my ________ name is Lucy. She's great. My ________ names are Dave and Cathy. My ________ names are Tom and Rose.

3116

[1] Your mother.

17 What's wrong? (Possessive form) ▸ p. 41 • GF 9 (p. 138)

Write the sentences again. Where is there an ***'s*** *or an* ***s'****?*

The Thompsons, Jo and Dan s grandparents, are at the Shaw s house. Dan and Jo s mum is the Thompson s daughter Catherine. Dan s favourite uncle is Catherine s brother Harry.
Dan and Jo have got three cousins too. Anne is Dan s f avourite cousin and Mark is Jo s favourite cousin.

____

____

____

____

____

3217 ____

Just for fun

Ken's father is Rob's son, so Rob is Ken's ...[1]

18 Our pet photos (Possessive determiners) ▸ p. 41 • GF 8 (p. 138)

Complete with: ***my, your, his, her, its, our, your, their***

1 *Jack* Look. That's me with ______ parrot. ______ name is Polly.

2 *Sophie* We've got a hamster. Look. Here it is in ______ cage.

3 *Toby* And here's a photo of ______ rabbits, Hip and Hop.

They are in ______ hutch.

Sophie This is Toby with ______ favourite rabbit, Hip.

4 *Jo* Here we are with Bill and Ben.

Ananda Oh! They're ______ cats. Great! I like cats.

5 *Sophie* This is ______ cousin Emma with ______ tortoise.

3218 6 *Ananda* ______ cousin has got a tortoise? What's ______ name?

[1] ... grandfather.

19 READING Tim's Saturday ▸ p. 49

a) *Look at the pictures. Then read the texts. Match the texts to the pictures.*

1 ☐

2 ☐

3 ☐

4 ☐

A

Before bed, Tim listens to rap music in his room. Barnabas sits in his favourite place, on Tim's bed, and watches TV. Then he sleeps again – his favourite activity.

B

Tim does tricks on his skateboard. Barnabas sits and watches the birds. He doesn't climb trees. That's lots of work – and Barnabas doesn't like work. At lunch time the friends don't go home. They eat sandwiches in the park.

C

Saturday is Tim's favourite day. He gets up at nine and has breakfast with his family. Barnabas has breakfast too. He likes lots of cat food – but he thinks the Baxters don't give him enough.

D

Tim goes to the park and meets his friends there. Barnabas likes an easy life, so Tim pulls him on his skateboard. Tim's friends laugh, and Barnabas is happy.

b) *What goes together? Match and write under the correct text in a).*

A great place for a good time | Lunch in the park | Breakfast with the family | The end of the day

3319

20 My dream house

▸ p. 50–51

a) *Read and choose words for your text. Mark your words with a felt tip.*

My dream house is a/an  old / new / big / little  flat. / house. / houseboat. / treehouse.

It's in  Germany. / England. / Australia. / New Zealand. / India. It has got a  park / garden and there are lots of  trees. / birds. / rabbits. / horses. / parrots.

My dream house has got  lots of / twelve / six / three / … rooms.

 Upstairs / Downstairs there's a/ there are  living room(s). / kitchen(s). / bedroom(s). / bathroom(s). / dining room(s).

b) *Use the text and words in a) and write about your dream house.*

My dream house is ______________________________

____

3420 ______________________________

c) *Now write about the things in the rooms. Choose from the box.*

there's a/an there are lots of/ two/ten/…	nice/big/great old/… red/blue/green/ orange/…	armchair • dishwasher • desk • bed • TV • lamp • wardrobe • posters • chairs • table • bath • sofa • fridge • cooker • sink • shower • computer • pictures • shelves • stereo • washing machine

In the kitchen there's a ______________________________

____

In the bathroom there ______________________________

____

In my bedroom there ______________________________

____

1 What are they? Label the pets.

1 ______________ 4 ______________

2 ______________ 5 ______________

3 ______________ 6 ______________

2 *'s* or *s'*?

1 The (Kapoors) ______________ flat is over the shop.

2 7PK is (Mr Kingsley) ______________ form.

3 Bill and Ben are (Dan and Jo) ______________ pets.

4 Barnabas is (Tim) ______________ cat.

3 *His*, *her*, *its* or *their*?

1 The Carter-Browns and all ______________ pets are at home today.

2 Prunella is at home. Sophie's room is ______________ room too.

3 Jack is in the park with ______________ dad.

4 Sophie's cousin Emma has got a tortoise. What's ______________ name?

4 Complete the sentences with: *like*, *likes* (✓), *doesn't like*, *don't like* (✗)

	horses	fish	cats
Lucy	✓	✓	✗
Jo	✓	✗	✓
Tim	✓	✗	✓
Florian	✓	✗	✗
Becky	✓	✓	✓

1 Lucy ______________ horses and fish. She ______________ cats.

2 Jo and Tim ______________ fish, but they ______________ horses and cats.

3 Florian ______________ fish or cats.

4 Becky ______________ all the pets.

20 points

Now you

Write three sentences about pets: I've got a ... / My friend/cousin has got a ... His/Her name is ... I like/I don't like ...

____

____

____

____

3505
3506
3507

Unit 3 Sports and hobbies

1 WORDS Sports and hobbies ► pp. 52–53

Write lists of Form 7PK's sports and hobbies.

play football · play computer games · go swimming · collect stamps · play hockey · make models · go riding · play the guitar

Sports

The students ...

play football

____

____

____

Hobbies

The students ...

play computer games

____

____

____

3601

2 REVISION Sophie goes riding ... (Simple present: statements) ► p. 53 • GF 7 (pp. 136–137)

Complete the sentences. Use the words in exercise 1.

Sophie	√					x
Ananda	x			√		
Dan and Jo	x	x	√	√		
Jack		x	√		x	√

1 Sophie *goes* riding, but she *doesn't make* models.

2 Ananda ____________ swimming, but she ____________ riding.

3 Jack ____________ models, but he ____________ the guitar.

4 Dan and Jo ____________ swimming, but they ____________ riding.

3602 5 Dan, Jo and Jack ____________ computer games, but they ____________ stamps.

Now you

Write about your sports and hobbies.

I ____________________________

____________, but I ____________.

3 WORDS A picture puzzle ► p. 54

a) *Complete the picture puzzle.*

► 1	_ _ _ _ _
2	_ _ _ _ _
3	_ _ _ _ _
4	_ _ _ _ _ _
5	_ _ _ _ _
6	_ _ _ _ _
7	_ – _ _ _ _ _

b) *Now complete the sentences about Florian with words from a).*

3703

Florian plays in a football team. Look, he's got a red and white ______________ and red ______________.

His football ______________ are black and white and his ______________ are white.

4 Do you play ...? (Simple present: questions and short answers) ► p. 54 • GF 10a–b (p. 139)

Write questions. Then write short answers: ***Yes, I do. / No, I don't.***

1 Do you *play football*?
____

2 Do you ______________?
____

3 Do ______________?
____

4 ______________
____

5 ______________
____

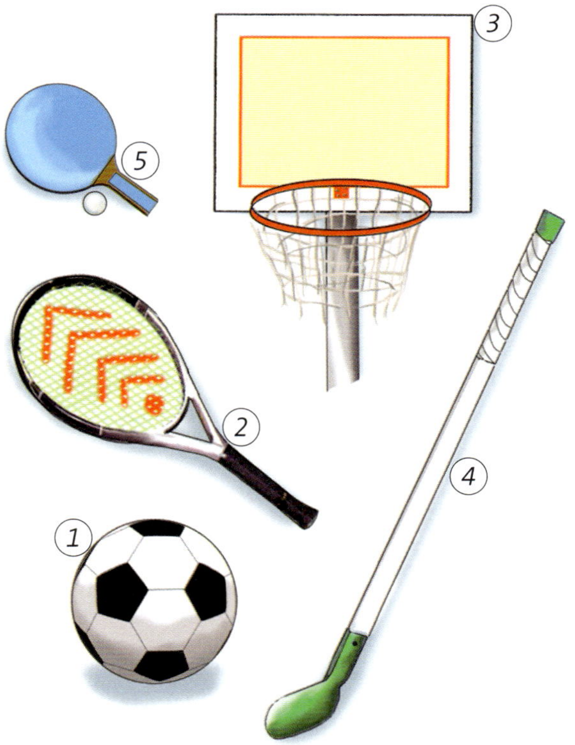

5 Weekends (Simple present: questions)

▸ p. 54a • GF 10a (p. 139)

Write questions with words from the pink and blue boxes. Then tick (√) the yellow boxes.

read • listen • *go* • play • meet

1 ... to the shops?
2 ... to music?
3 ... the guitar?
4 ... your friends?
5 ... comics in bed?

Weekends	☺	☹
Do you *go to the shops*?		
Do you ____________?		
Do ____________?		
____________		
____________		

6 Ananda's hockey shoes (Simple present: questions and short answers)

▸ p. 54 • GF 10a–b (p. 139)

Complete the questions with **do** *or* **does**. *Then write answers:* **Yes, she does. / No, they don't. / ...**

1 *Does* Ananda need hockey shoes? Yes, *she does*.
2 *Do* Ananda and her mum need a shop assistant? Yes, ____________.
3 ________ size four fit? Yes, ____________.
4 ________ Ananda like the colour? No, ____________.
5 ________ she try on red and white shoes? Yes, ____________.
3806 6 ________ Ananda and her mum take T-shirts too? No, ____________.

● 7 Free time (Simple present: questions)

▸ p. 54 • GF 10a (p. 139)

Write questions.

1 Jo likes sport. (And Jack?)
Does Jack like sport?

2 Prunella collects plates. (And Sophie?)
____

3 Ananda and Sophie go swimming. (And Dan and Jo?)
____

4 Ananda plays hockey. (And Prunella?)
____

5 Jack makes models. (And Dan and Jo?)
____

8 What does Ananda ask? (Simple present: wh-questions)

▸ p. 55 • GF 10c (p. 140)

Complete her questions with: **What**, **When**, **Where**

Rhyme time

I've got two hamsters,
Kim and Kay,
They've got a big cage
With lots of hay[1].
They play all night and sleep all day –
But because they're hamsters,
That's OK.

Ananda's questions:		Sophie's answers:
1 What	do Hip and Hop eat?	Lots of carrots.
2 ______	do they play?	In the garden.
3 ______	do they sleep?	At night.
4 ______	do they drink?	Just water.

9 STUDY SKILLS Wörter nachschlagen

▸ p. 55 • SF 4 (p. 126)

a) *The boxes are full of Sophie's old things. Write the words in alphabetical order.*

photos • books • posters • boxes • pictures • packets of stamps • CDs • calendars • balls • comics • birthday cards • computer games

Just for fun

Where does Thursday come before Wednesday?[2]

b) *Add the following words to the list of p-words in a):* **pens**, **pencils**, **poems**. *Where do they go? Check with the Dictionary in your student's book.*

packets of stamps, ______

3909

[1] hay [heɪ] *Heu* [2] In the dictionary.

10 PRONUNCIATION [æ] and [eɪ] ▸ p. 56 4

*Listen to the words. Where are the [æ]-sounds, like **cat**? Where are the [eɪ]-sounds, like **snake**? Colour the **cat**-words **red** and the **snake**-words **blue**.*

4010

cat	snake	flat
bag	plate	day
late	rabbit	black
make	back	table
stamp	act	plan
say	lamp	place

11 WORDS Pairs ▸ p. 56

a) *Which words go together? Find, colour and write opposites.*

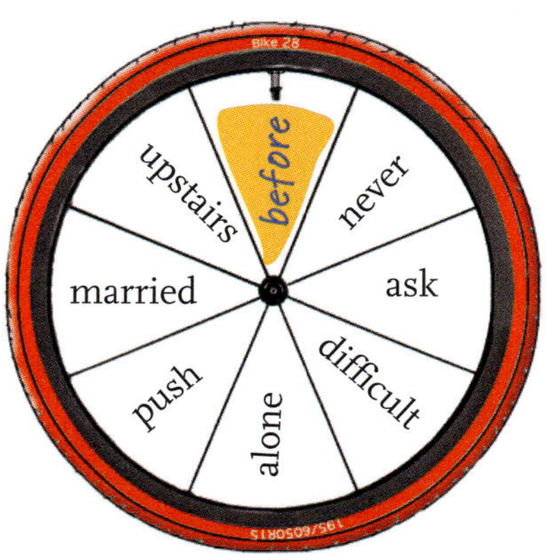

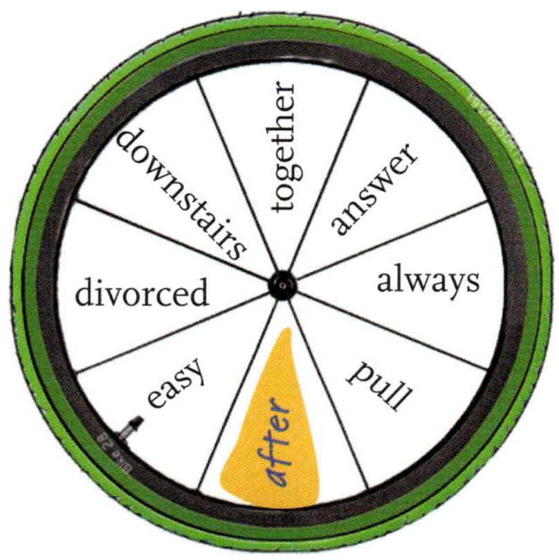

before – after

______ – ______

______ – ______

______ – ______

______ – ______

______ – ______

______ – ______

______ – ______

b) *Complete with words from a).*

Prunella ______ plays tennis with Uncle Henry. He ______ wins because he hasn't got a head. He likes the old house, but it looks different ______ 100 years. Sophie and Prunella's room is ______. ______, in the living room, there's a piano. Prunella can play. It's ______ with a head, but it's ______ for poor Uncle Henry.

12 Sentence snakes (Adverbs: word order) ► p. 56 • GF 11 (p. 140)

Cross out the wrong word. Colour the correct word. Then write the sentence.

1 

We always get up early.

2 

____

3 

____

4 

____

5 

____

13 About Tim (Adverbs: word order) ► p. 56 • GF 11 (p. 140)

Write sentences about Tim.

Does he …?	always	usually	often	sometimes	never
1 help at home?				√	
2 go to football matches?	√				
3 get up before 7 o'clock?					√
4 watch TV after school?		√			
5 go to bed late?			√		

1 Tim sometimes helps at home.

2 He ________________________________.

3 ________________________________

4 ________________________________

4113 5 ________________________________

Now you

*What do you **always**, **sometimes** or **never** do at the weekend? Write three sentences.*

I always ______________________________

____

____

Just for fun

A: I often play computer games with my dog.
B: Wow! You've got a very clever pet.
A: Not really. I always win.

14 WORDS *Go*, *play* or *do*?

▸ p. 57

a) *Match, then write.*

badminton · swimming · hockey · judo · yoga · tennis · basketball · dancing · riding

go · play · do

go swimming, ______________________________

play ______________________________

do ______________________________

b) *Now complete Toby's sentences with the correct form of **go**, **play** or **do**.*

Do you __________ football or basketball? In our family we all like sport. I __________ judo. Emily __________ tennis. Sophie likes horses, so she __________ riding. In summer we all __________ swimming. Mum __________ yoga – and my dad watches sport on TV.

4214

15 What do they have to do? (have to/has to)

▸ p. 57 • GF 12 (p. 141)

Write four sentences.

Ananda The students in 7PK Jack Sophie and Toby	has to have to	feed Sheeba and the other pets. lay the tables at the B&B. help in the shop. do an English project.

1 Ananda has to ______________________________.

2 ______________________________

3 ______________________________

4 ______________________________

16 Who has to do what? (have to/has to) ▸ p. 57 • GF 12 (p. 141)

*Write sentences with **have to**, **has to**, **don't have to** or **doesn't have to**. Choose from the box.*

> *do his Maths homework* • go to her piano lesson • clean his bike • get up early • make his bed • clean the kitchen

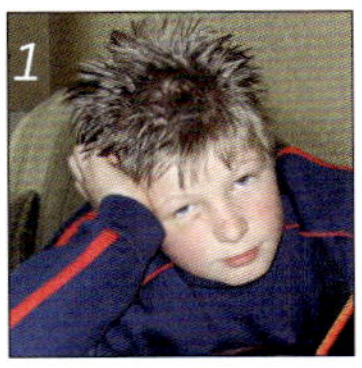
1 Florian

4 Becky

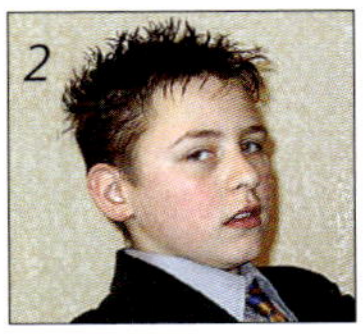
2 Tim

5 Tim and Becky

3 Becky and Tim

6 Florian

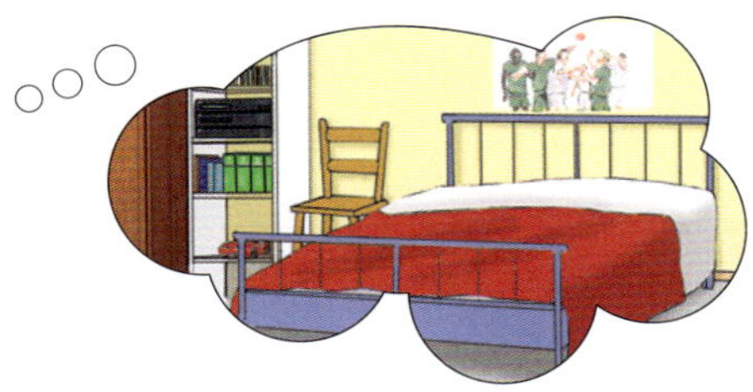

1 *Florian has to do his Maths homework.*

2 ______________________________

3 ______________________________

4 ______________________________

5 ______________________________

4316 6 ______________________________

Now you

What do you have to do every day? Write two sentences.

____

____

What don't you have to do every day? Write two sentences.

____

____

17 WORKING WITH THE TEXT The SHoCK Team ▸ pp. 65–66

a) *Read pp. 65–66 in your student's book again. Match the text to the pictures. Write the letters A–F in the boxes.*

1

2

3

4

5

6

A He sees a scary man in black outside Mr Green's room.

B Jack is alone in his room.

C The man runs outside. Jack can't see him on the street.

D Suddenly there's a noise, so he looks downstairs.

E They say he has to tell the police or his parents.

F Jack tells his friends about the scary man in black.

b) *Who thinks what? Match the bubbles to the friends in the SHoCK Team.*

I've got an idea. I need a piece of paper.

I've got a piece of paper. Here it is.

Jack has to tell his parents about the man in black.

We all have to watch Mr Green.

Yes! 'Detective Jo Shaw'...

Jack has to call the police.

Ananda

Sophie

Jack

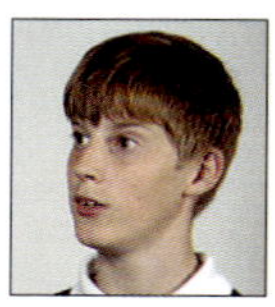
Dan

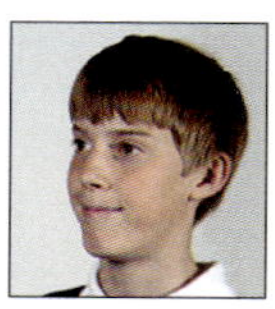
Jo

● ***c)*** *Write answers.*

1 Does the man in black go into Mr Green's room?

____

2 What does Jack think about Mr Green?

____

3 What do the children have to do?

____

d) *In the History lesson, Jack writes a code message*[1] *to the SHoCK Team. What does it say?*

1	2	3	4	5	6	7	8	9	10	11	12	13	14	15	16	17	18	19	20	21	22	23	24	25	26
A	B	C	D	E	F	G	H	I	J	K	L	M	N	O	P	Q	R	S	T	U	V	W	X	Y	Z

23 8 5 18 5   4 15 5 19   13 18   7 18 5 5 14   7 15   1 6 20 5 18

_ _ _ _ _   _ _ _ _   _ _   _ _ _ _ _   _ _   _ _ _ _ _

2 18 5 1 11 6 1 19 20?   23 5   8 1 22 5   20 15   6 9 14 4   15 21 20!

_ _ _ _ _ _ _ _ _ ?   _ _   _ _ _ _   _ _   _ _ _ _   _ _ _ !

[1] code message [kəʊd 'mesɪdʒ] *verschlüsselte Nachricht*

Activity page 1

Word pairs ▸ Welcome · Unit 1 · Topic 1

- *Cut out the parts.*
- *Put the pairs together.*
- *What have you got?*

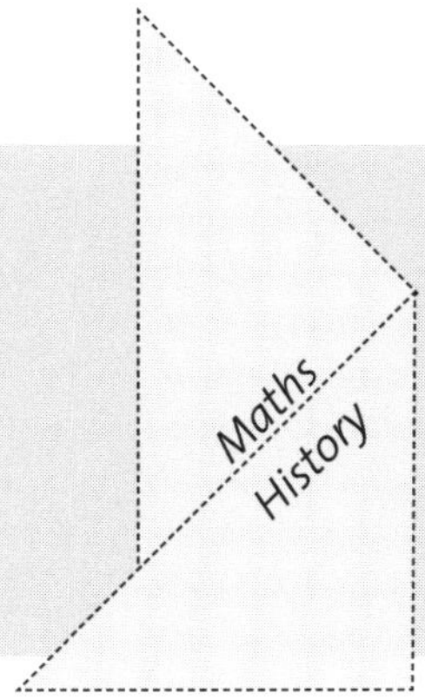

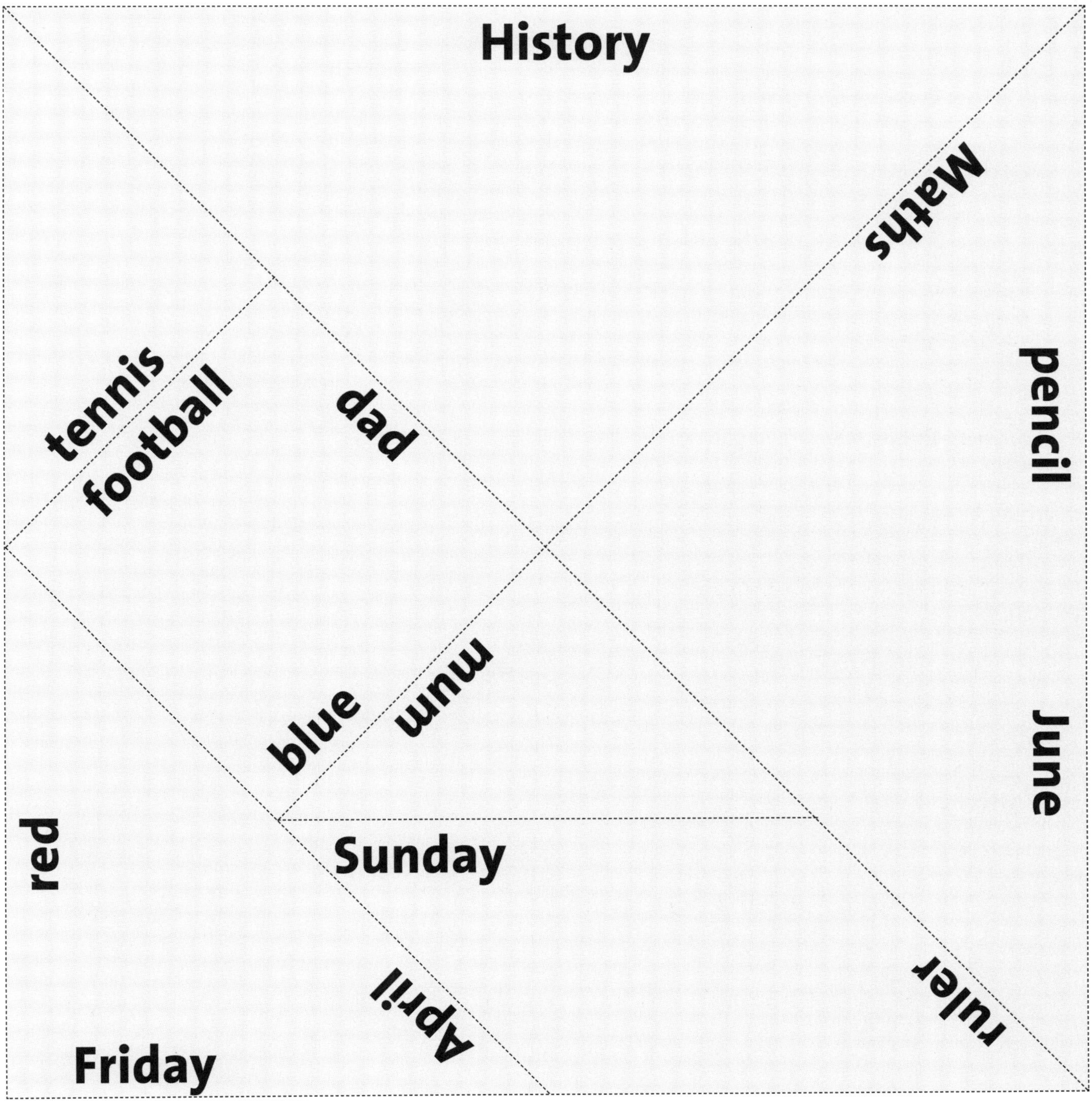

Activity page 2

British money Topic 3 *(p. 67)*

- *Cut out the money.*
- *Glue the correct parts.*
- *How much money is there?*
- *You can act with this money in your jumble sale.*

Activity page 3

Food memory game ▸ Unit 4

- *Cut out the word cards and the pictures.*
- *Put the cards on the table, so that you can't see the words and the pictures.*
- *Take two cards and match the correct picture and the word card. Go on!*
- *You can play this game with a partner.*

	a birthday cake		a plate of cheese	
ice cream		potatoes		sausages
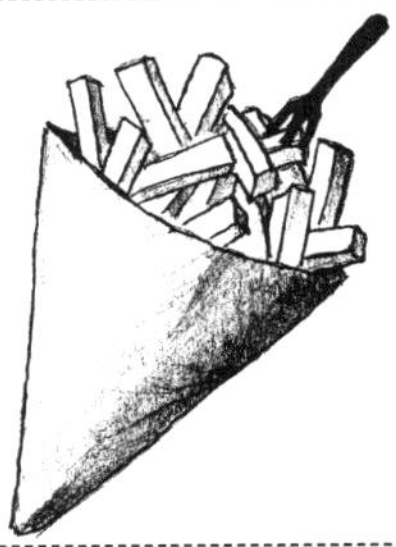	a piece of cake		a jug of milk	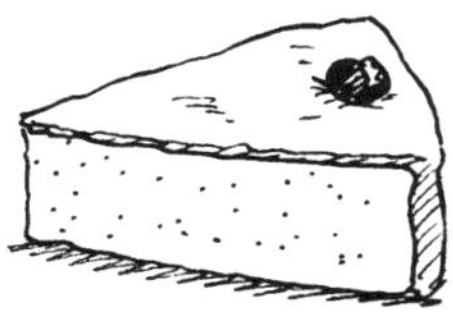
a bowl of salad		a glass of orange juice		a packet of crisps
	chips		chicken	
sweets		sandwiches		a bottle of cola

Activity page 4

A Christmas card

Topic 6 *(p. 113)*

- *Cut out the Christmas card and cut out the three sides of the little window.*
- *Cut out the picture of the sock. Put glue on the sides.*
- *Glue the picture of the sock in the window.*
- *Cut out Merry Christmas. Put the two words at the top of the card.*
- *Colour the card.*

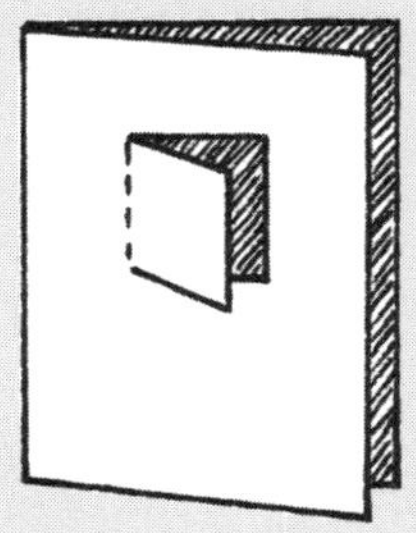

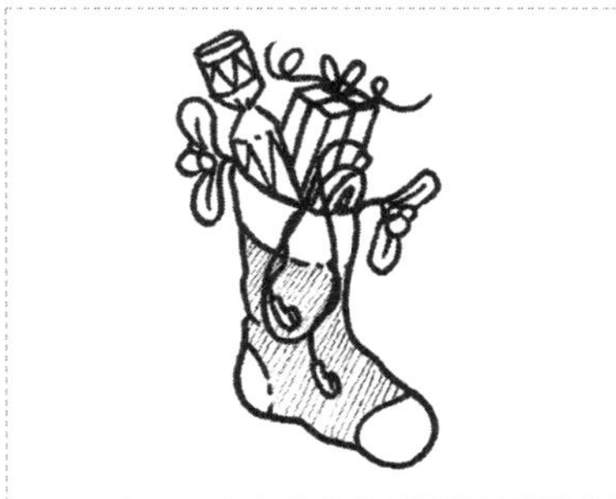

18 In the Oxfam shop ▸ p. 67

a) *How much is it? Write the prices on the things in the Oxfam shop.*

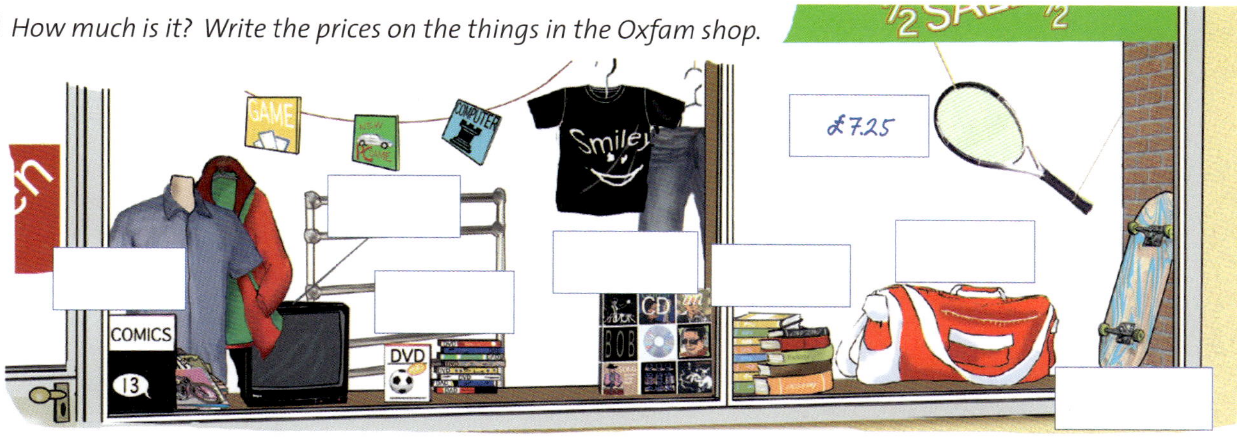

The tennis racket is seven pounds twenty-five.
The bag is six pounds fifty.
4518 The CDs are two pounds eighty-five each[1].
The comics are seventy p each.
The computer games are five pounds each.
The DVDs are three pounds forty-nine each.
The skateboard is ten pounds ninety-nine.
The books are two pounds sixty each.

b) *Jo is in the Oxfam shop. What does Jo say? Write* J. *What does the shop assistant say? Write* A. *Then write correct sentences in the speech bubbles.*

___ Oh, then I'll take it. Here's the money.
A Hello. Can I help you?
___ Let's see. It's £10.99.
___ And here's your change. Thank you.
___ Oh, that's too much.
___ How much is the bag?
___ Mmm. I've only got £6.50 and 25p is for the bus.
___ The bag is £6.50.
J Yes, how much is the skateboard, please?
___ Mmm. Well, I can take 25p off.
___ Thank you. Bye.

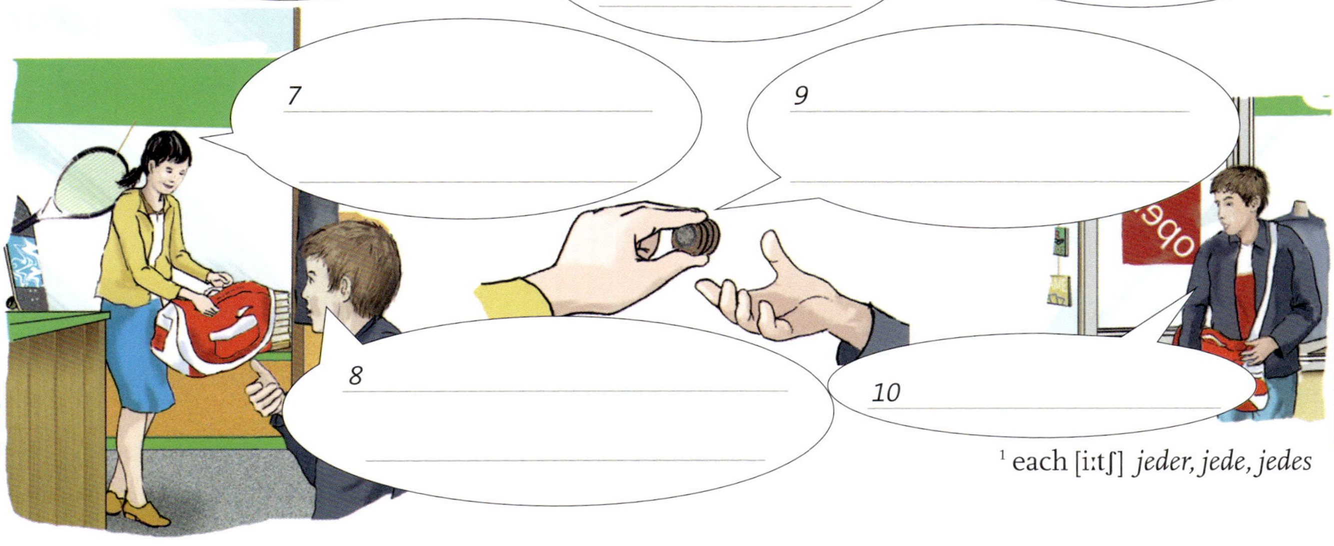

4519
4520

[1] each [iːtʃ] *jeder, jede, jedes*

1 Sports and hobbies

*Use **collect**, **go**, **make**, **play** and complete the sentences.*

1 Jack ______________________.

2 Sophie ______________________.

3 Dilip ______________________.

4 Ananda ______________________.

2 Ask about the people in ( ).

1 Jo and Jack like music. (Dan and Sophie?) ______________________

2 Prunella plays tennis. (Sophie?) ______________________

3 Ananda writes e-mails. (you?) ______________________

4 Jack's mum does yoga. (Jack's dad?) ______________________

3 Make correct sentences.

1 goes/never/Jay/to football matches ______________________

2 write/I/don't/often/e-mails ______________________

3 Becky/play/does/basketball ? ______________________

4 does/Prunella/tennis/play/where ? ______________________

4 Write what they *have to* do or *don't have to* do.

1 At school we ______________ listen to the teacher.

2 Most days Jack ______________ help at the B&B.

3 In the holidays we ______________ get up early.

4 Prunella ______________ go to school.

16 points

Now you

Write four sentences about sports and hobbies. Do you play football or tennis? Do you collect or make things? What about your friends and family?

____

____

____

4605
4606

Jetzt kann ich ...

	Sehr gut!	OK	Verbessern!
HÖREN: Ich kann ...			
... die Arbeitsanweisungen und Fragen im Unterricht verstehen.	☐	☐	☐
... Fragen über mich, meine Familie, Haustiere und Freizeit verstehen.	☐	☐	☐
... die Hörtexte der Units 1–3 verstehen.	☐	☐	☐
SPRECHEN: Ich kann ...			
... jemanden begrüßen, mich vorstellen und mich verabschieden.	☐	☐	☐
... jemanden nach dem Alter fragen und fragen, woher er/sie kommt.	☐	☐	☐
... über mich, meine Freunde, Familie und Freizeit sprechen.	☐	☐	☐
... über Haustiere und ihre Behausungen sprechen.	☐	☐	☐
... ein einfaches Einkaufsgespräch führen.	☐	☐	☐
... die Wörter der Units 1–3 richtig aussprechen.	☐	☐	☐
LESEN: Ich kann ...			
... die Arbeitsanweisungen in meinem Buch/Workbook verstehen.	☐	☐	☐
... die Texte und Dialoge der Units 1–3 lesen und verstehen.	☐	☐	☐
SCHREIBEN: Ich kann ...			
... Wörter und kurze Sätze richtig abschreiben.	☐	☐	☐
... über mich, meine Freunde, Familie, Haustiere und Freizeit schreiben.	☐	☐	☐
... über unsere Wohnung/unser Haus/verschiedene Zimmer schreiben.	☐	☐	☐
... über meinen Tagesablauf schreiben.	☐	☐	☐
... Wörter für Familienmitglieder und Verwandte richtig schreiben.	☐	☐	☐
... schreiben, wem etwas gehört. Dazu verwende ich *'s* oder *s'*.	☐	☐	☐
LAND UND LEUTE: Ich weiß, ...			
... wie der Schultag britischer Schülerinnen und Schüler aussieht.	☐	☐	☐
... wie britische Schülerinnen und Schüler ihre Freizeit verbringen.	☐	☐	☐
LERNEN UND ARBEITEN: Ich kann ...			
... in meinem Buch Vokabeln und Grammatikregeln nachschlagen.	☐	☐	☐
... mithilfe von Vorgaben ein Vokabelnetzwerk oder eine Mindmap ergänzen.	☐	☐	☐
... mit meiner Lieblingsmethode Vokabeln selbstständig lernen.	☐	☐	☐
... mit einem Partner oder einer Partnerin und in einer Gruppe arbeiten.	☐	☐	☐

WIE ICH MICH VERBESSERN KÖNNTE: Ich könnte ...

... meinen Karteikasten häufiger benutzen.	☐	... schwierige Wörter häufiger abschreiben.	☐
... Texte aus meinem Buch zu Hause laut lesen.	☐	... kurze Texte abschreiben.	☐
... Texte aus meinem Buch auswendig lernen.	☐	... Dialoge mit Freunden üben.	☐

Unit 4 Party, party!

1 WORDS Sophie's shopping list ▸ pp. 68–69

a) *Write Sophie's shopping list of food and drinks for the party.*

chocolate cake • carrots • cheese • chicken • chips • biscuits • cola • crisps • fruit • ice cream • lemonade • orange juice • sausages • sweets

1 
2 
3 
4 
5 
6 
7 
8 
9 
10 
11 
12 
13 
14 

Shopping list

1 ______	8 ______
2 ______	9 ______
3 ______	10 ______
4 ______	11 ______
5 ______	12 ______
6 ______	13 ______
7 ______	14 ______

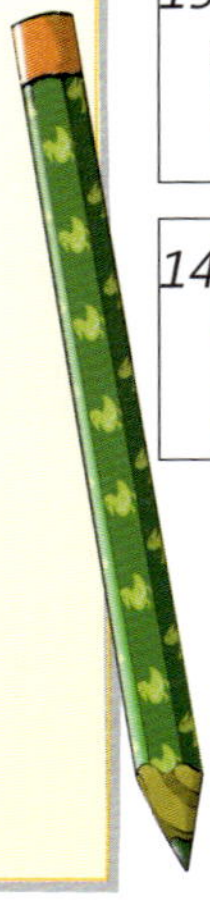

b) *Draw and label your favourite party food. Choose three things.*

chicken • sausages • fruit salad • chocolate cake • ice cream • carrot salad • hamburgers

______ ______ ______

4801

Now you

What food and drinks do you like? What don't you like?

I like ______.

I don't like ______.

2 WORDS What's on the table? ▸ p. 69

Match words from the boxes. Write: a plate of ..., a bottle of ...

bowl • bottle • basket • *plate* • jug

cheese • fruit • milk • orange juice • cornflakes

1 *a plate of cheese*

2 ______________________

3 ______________________

4 ______________________

4902 5 ______________________

3 Would you like some tea? ▸ p. 69

Complete Becky's questions and Florian's answers.

1  2  3  4 

1 *Becky:* Would you *like some tea*?

2 *Florian:* No, thank you. But I ______________________.

3 *Becky:* And would ______________________?

4903 4 *Florian:* No, __________. But ______________________.

4 An invitation ▸ p. 70

Florian invites Becky and Tim to a barbecue. What does the invitation say? Look at p. 70 of your student's book again. Then complete the text.

Florian's *barbecue*

__________ Becky and Tim

__________ come __________ my barbecue!

__________? At 24 Gordon Road

When? __________ Saturday, 16th April

Time? __________ 2.30

5 Sophie's party (Subject and object pronouns) ▸ p. 70 • GF 13 (p. 141)

a) Match and colour.

Rhyme time

Friends and invitations,
Cake and ice cream too.
I ♥ birthdays,
What about you?

b) Now complete with: **me, you, him, her, it, us, them**

1 *Sophie* Birthday parties are great. I really like ______________.

2 *Prunella* Would you like a nice cake from ______________? We can make ______________ together.

3 *Sophie* Prunella, I really can't invite ______________ to my party. I'm sorry.

4 *Prunella* Well, Uncle Henry likes parties. Can you invite ______________? No, you can't.

You can't invite ______________ because we aren't real people. Right?

5005

But Ananda can come. You like ______________ – and she's real.

6 Invitations (Object pronouns for German 'sie') ▸ p. 70 • GF 13 (p. 141)

Find and circle the correct word.

1 *Sophie* Where's my invitation list, Prunella? I can't find (them/it/her).

2 *Prunella* Have Dan and Jo got an invitation? You like (her/them/it).

What about your cousin Emma? Have you got (it/her/them) on your list?

And what about all the neighbours' children?

3 *Sophie* No, I really can't invite (her/it/them). They make too much noise.

Prunella Right – and they eat too much.

Sophie Prunella!

7 STUDY SKILLS Notizen machen

▸ p. 71 • SF 5 (p. 127)

Mark the key words, then write them.
The SHoCK Team meets after school.

Jack OK, SHoCK Team detectives. We have to find out about Mr Green. Who can do what?
Sophie I can write down our ideas.
Jo We can follow him at weekends. I can start tomorrow. I can be at the B&B at 8.30. What about you, Dan?
Dan Yes, great, and what about some photos of Mr Green?
Ananda Maybe I can find out about bank robbers in the computer.
Jack Great idea! And I can follow Mr Green on my bike on Sunday.
Dan Then we can all meet on Sunday evening. OK?
Jack OK, let's meet in the park at six o'clock.

5107

SHoCK Team – Ideas
Find out about Mr Green

Jo – follow – weekends
– start tomorrow
– B&B – 8.30

Dan ______

Ananda ______
______

Jack ______
______

Dan ______
______

Jack ______

8 Some sausages and some milk (some and any)

▸ p. 71 • GF 14 (p. 142)

Tim and Becky go shopping for their mum.

Shopping list
milk
cheese
sausages
crisps
ice cream
biscuits

a) *What have Tim and Becky got in their baskets? Use* **some**.

Becky has got some milk, some ______,
______ and ______.

Tim has got ______, ______
______ and ______.

b) *Which three things haven't they got? Use* **any**.

They haven't got ______, ______ or ______.

9 Tim's birthday list (some and any) ▸ p. 71 • GF 14 (p. 142)

What does Tim want for his birthday? Look at the list. Use **some** *and* **any**.

✓ posters
✗ books
✓ CDs
✗ hockey shoes
✗ socks
✓ money
✓ chocolate
✓ other sweets

5209

1 He wants *some* posters, but he doesn't want *any* books.

2 He wants ______ CDs, but he doesn't want ______.

3 He doesn't want ______, but he wants ______.

4 Does he want ______ chocolate?

5 And does he want ______? – Yes, he does.

Now you

What do you want for your next birthday? Use **some** *and* **any**.

I want ______,

but I don't want ______.

10 WORDS The mad computer ▸ p. 71

○ ***a)*** *The mad computer sometimes writes wrong letters. Write the words with the correct letters.*

?nv?t&t?#n	f%nny	∫xp∫ns?v∫	b#r?ng
______	______	______	______

pr∫s∫nt	s%ngl&ss∫s	d?ff?c%lt
______	______	______

b) *Now put the correct words from a) in Ananda's e-mail to Jack.*

Hi, Jack!

I've got an ______ to Sophie's party too. I've got an idea. Let's buy her a ______ together – not too ______ because I haven't got much money – maybe a ______ present? It's ______. Not soap or chocolate. That's ______.

Have you got any ideas? What about some ______? See you at school.

Ananda

11 At the Baxters' (Present progressive: positive statements)

▸ p. 72 • GF 15a–b (pp. 142–143)

It's two o'clock on Sunday afternoon. What are the Baxters doing? Make sentences.

Barnabas Mrs Baxter Mr Baxter Grandma and Grandpa Tim and Florian Becky and Lucy	is are	tidying sleeping cleaning watching playing making	the living room. a computer game. a mess. TV. the cooker. on the sofa.

1 Barnabas is sleeping on the sofa.

2 Mrs Baxter is cleaning .

3

4

5

5311 6

12 Where are the verbs? (-ing-forms)

▸ p. 72 • GF 15b (p. 143)

a) *Find and write nine verbs.*

F	E	E	D	K	S	T
O	S	R	U	N	J	A
L	W	R	I	T	E	K
L	I	Y	G	I	V	E
O	M	K	E	G	E	T
W	A	L	K	K	I	L

feed

b) *Now write the verbs in the correct list.*

+ ing	~~e~~ + ing	double letter + ing
feed – feeding	take – taking	swim – swimming

13 Becky's dream birthday (Present progressive: positive statements) ► p. 72 • GF 15b (p. 143)

Becky is thinking about her dream birthday. What's happening? Choose verbs from the box.

dance • drink • eat • give • have • play • sing • sit • swim • talk

I'm having a big barbecue at my dream house.

We ____________ chicken and hamburgers and we ____________ banana juice. All my friends ____________ me lots of presents. My favourite band ____________ really great music. Now I ____________ with my favourite pop star. Tim ____________ at the swimming pool[1]. He ____________ to some Hollywood stars. Some of the guests ____________ in the pool. Now my favourite film stars ____________ 'Happy birthday to Becky'… It's my dream party!

5413

14 Prunella's visitor (Present progressive: positive and negative statements) ► p. 72 • GF 15b (p. 143)

Prunella has got a visitor. It's Uncle Henry. What are they doing in the pictures?
Write two sentences for each picture.

1 It's 2.30.
Is Prunella making sandwiches or is she making tea?
She isn't making tea. She's making sandwiches.

2 It's 3 o'clock.
Is Uncle Henry listening to music or is he watching TV?
____

3 It's 3.15.
Are they reading newspapers or are they looking at old photos?
____
____

4 It's 3.30.
Is Prunella playing the piano or is she dancing?
____

5 Now it's 4 o'clock.
Are they eating ice cream or are they having sandwiches and tea?
____
____

[1] swimming pool ['swɪmɪŋ pu:l] *Schwimmbecken*

15 Questions and answers (Present progressive: questions and short answers) ▸ p. 74 • GF 15c (p. 143)

*Write questions. Then look at exercise 14 and write short answers: **Yes, she is. / No, ...***

1 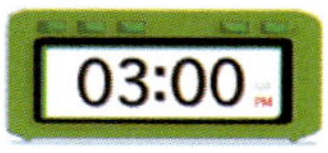

Uncle Henry/newspapers/reading/is ?

____

2 

looking/at old photos/are/Prunella and Uncle Henry ?

____

____

3 

Prunella/playing/is/the piano?

____

Just for fun

A: What are you doing?
B: I'm eating this cake.
A: But that's **my** cake.
B: OK. Then I'm eating **your** cake.

Now you

What are you and your family doing now? Write in your exercise book:
My mum/dad/sister/brother/ ... is/are ... doing/...

16 PRONUNCIATION [əʊ] or [ɒ]? ▸ p. 74 5

Which words are like ***phone*** *[əʊ] and which are like* ***sock*** *[ɒ]? Listen to the words and match.*

5516

phone [əʊ]

poster, clock, hockey, home, bottle, old, hobby, yoga, bowl, comic, boat, alone, box

sock [ɒ]

17 GETTING BY IN ENGLISH Florian's cousin ▸ p. 74

Florian's cousin Heike is in Bristol. They're at Tim's house. What does Florian say?

Tim Would Heike like a drink?

Florian *Möchtest du etwas trinken?*

Heike Ja, bitte. Ich möchte Orangensaft.

Florian Yes, ____________ . She would ____________ some ____________ .

Tim Would she like a cheese sandwich or some potato salad?

Florian Möchtest du ______________________________ ?

Heike Ich möchte bitte ein Käsebrot und etwas Kartoffelsalat.

Florian Oh. She ______________________________ .

Tim Well, OK.

18 READING Tim's party ▸ p. 82

a) *Read about Tim's birthday party. Write the names of his friends in the picture.*

It's Tim's 12th birthday. Look, he's having a disco with all his friends. I'm here too – but Tim doesn't know that. I haven't got an invitation, so I'm hiding ... Can you see me? The party room is great. There's a table with presents – and lots of food. There isn't any cat food, but there's some chicken, some fish, some sausages ...
What are the party guests doing? Well, a DJ is playing the music. His name is Tony. Tim is talking to him. Pat and Jill are looking at the presents. Pat is the girl with long hair. Sue is dancing with Florian. She's wearing jeans and a nice red T-shirt – my favourite colour. Ed and Alex are eating sandwiches. Ed is drinking lemonade too. Ali is telling funny jokes and Gina is laughing. Lucy has got her guitar with her. Great – she isn't playing it. She's bad, but the DJ's music is cool. Mmm. They aren't looking. Yes, now is a good time ...

Twenty minutes later ...
Ed Where's the fish? The plate is empty.
Ali There isn't any chicken. Where is it all?
Sue And who's got all the sausages?

● ***b)*** *Now complete the sentences.*

1 Tim is having a disco because it's ______________________.

2 Barnabas hasn't got an invitation, so ______________________.

3 In the party room there's a big table with ______________________.

4 Sue is wearing ______________________.

5 Gina is laughing because Ali ______________________.

6 Lucy has got her guitar with her, but she ______________________.

5618 7 Barnabas eats all the ______________________.

1 What does Mrs Carter-Brown need from the shops?

Write her shopping list.

1 ____________________
2 ____________________
3 ____________________
4 ____________________
5 ____________________
6 ____________________

2 Complete with: *me*, *him*, *her*, *it*, *them*

1 *Tim* Where's Mum's shopping list? I can't find ________ .

2 *Becky* I don't know. Don't ask ________ .

3 *Tim* Well, where's Mum? Let's ask ________ .

4 *Becky* Where are Mum and Dad? I can't see ________ .

5 *Tim* Dad is in the garden. Let's ask ________ .

3 What's in the fridge? *Some* or *any*?

1 *Tim* There's ________ fruit, but there aren't ________ carrots.

2 *Becky* And is there ________ milk?

3 *Tim* No, but there's ________ lemonade.

4 What*'s happening* at the station? Use: *call*, *get on*, *give*, *read*, *run*

1 A man ________________ a newspaper.

2 Two girls ________________ the train.

3 A boy ________________ somebody on his mobile.

4 A woman ________________ a girl some money.

5 Two boys ________________ to the train.

20 points

Now you

5705
5706

Think about your dream birthday party. What are you and your party guests doing? What's happening? For ideas look at exercises 13 (p. 54) and 18 (p. 56). Write a short text (about six sentences) in your exercise book.

Unit 5 School: not just lessons

1 WORDS Happy birthday, Grandpa ▸ p. 84–85

Oh no! Which words can't Jo's grandpa read? Write the words.

Choir • Computer • paint • pirates • practise • programmes • rehearsal • results • ship • *Spring*

Happy birthday, Grandpa!

It's our … Show next week. We have to p… a lot. I sing in the Junior …ir. My favourite song is about … My friend Ananda is in the Co…r Club. They're making the p…ra…s. Dan can…t so he's in the Art Club. They're painting a … for our pirate scene. We're all nervous. It's the last … on Tuesday. Sport is great too. Our Year 7 football …s are always good. That's all for now. Have a great birthday!

Jo – and Ben … Sorry!!

Spring, ______

______

______

______

______

______

______

2 WORDS School notice board ▸ pp. 84–85

The names of the clubs are wrong. Can you write the correct names?

1 **Dance Club**
Can you act in plays? We meet on Fridays after school, Room 10

2 **Junior Band**
Great result! Last match Wells 1 Cotham 3

3 **Drama Club**
Do you play the guitar or the clarinet? We meet on Mondays after school, Room 17

4 **Junior Choir**
Do you like dancing? Come to our club on Wednesday at 4pm, Room 20

5 **Art Club**
Can you sing? Come and sing with us. Thursdays, Room 17

6 **Football Team**
Can you paint pictures? We meet on Tuesdays after school, Room 11

1 *Drama Club*

2 ______

3 ______

4 ______

5 ______

6 ______

5802

3 An e-mail from Becky (was/were in positive statements)

► p. 86 • GF 17 (p. 144)

Here is an e-mail from Becky to her friend Lisa. Fill in **was** *or* **were**.

Hi, Lisa!

Last weekend I *was* at a party. My classmates *were* there too. The food ________ really great – so we ________ all very happy. There ________ some good salads and pizza. The music ________ fantastic (lots of noise!) – but the neighbours ________ OK because their kids ________ at the party too. ________ you at a party last weekend? ________ it a birthday party? Tell me about it!

Becky

4 Where were Tim's things? (was/were in positive and negative statements)

► p. 86 • GF 17 (p. 144)

Tim's room looks nice today. But where were his things yesterday?
Write sentences about Tim's things with **was**, **wasn't**, **were** *and* **weren't**.

Write about: 1 his shoes 2 his football 3 his comics 4 his clock 5 his school things

Tim's room today

Tim's room yesterday

1 *His shoes weren't* in the wardrobe. *They were* on the chair.

2 ________ on the wardrobe. ________ on the bed.

3 ________ on the shelf. ________ under the desk.

4 ________ on the table. ________ under the desk.

5 ________ on the desk. ________ on the bed.

5904

6 Barnabas ________ in his basket. He ________.

5 Saturday afternoon (was/were in questions and short answers) ▸ p. 86 • GF 17 (p. 144)

Where were they on Saturday afternoon? Write questions with **was** *or* **were** *and short answers:*
Yes, he was. / No, she wasn't. /…

1 Jo/at the sports shop?
Was Jo at the sports shop? – Yes, he was.

2 Sophie and Emily/at the cinema?
Were Sophie and Emily at the cinema? – No, they weren't. They were at the swimming pool.

3 Jack/at the pet shop?

4 Tim and Florian/at a football match?

5 Ananda/at the swimming pool?

6 Becky and Lucy/at home?

6005

• Now you

Where were you and your family (mum/dad/brother/sister) or your friends last Saturday afternoon? At the shops? At your grandma's house? … Write four sentences.

Last Saturday afternoon I was at ______________________

6 WORDS What are the words? ▸ p. 87

a) *Find and write the missing letters.*

ou | au | eo | ea | ei | oi | ai

reh *ea* rsal – sh__t – n__se – bec__se – w__t – r__dy

n__ghb__r – p__ple – s__nd – with__t – ch__r – upst__rs

b) *Now fill in correct forms from a).*

Jack: The ________ was fantastic. Our band played two songs ________ a mistake. Miss White says we ________ great. My parents can't ________ to see the show. Lots of ________ want to come, our ________ too. Jo sings in the ________. He makes lots of ________, and sings all the time.

6106

7 A verb snake (Simple past: regular verbs) ▸ p. 87 • GF 18a (p. 145)

Find and colour the verbs in the verb snake. Then write them in the simple past.

shouted, liked, ________

____

8 PRONUNCIATION Word CDs (Past forms) ▸ p. 87 • GF 18a (p. 145) 6

a) *Listen to the words. Where can you hear the extra syllable –ed* [ɪd]*? Colour the CDs* ***red*** *or* ***blue***.
Red = extra syllable: ***needed*** ['niːdɪd]. *Blue = no extra syllable:* ***called*** [kɔːld]

needed | called | painted 1 | worked 2 | added 3 | used 4

waited 5 | shouted 6 | watched 7 | started 8 | hated 9

b) *Now add the numbers of all the red CDs. Is your answer '32'? Correct!*

9 Last week (Simple past: regular verbs in positive statements)

▸ p. 87 • GF 18a (p. 145)

Look at Tim's notes for last week. Then write sentences.

Mon – clean dad's car ✓
Tue – walk to school – no bike ✓
Wed – help Alex with Maths ✓
Thur – call Florian and Ed ✓
Fri – watch DVDs with Florian ✓
Sat – play cards with Ed ✓

On Monday *he cleaned his dad's car.*

On Tuesday ______________________________.

On ______________________________.

____

____

____

10 Match the pieces (Simple past: irregular verbs in positive statements)

▸ p. 88 • GF 18b (p. 145)

○ **a)** *Find, colour and write the pairs.*

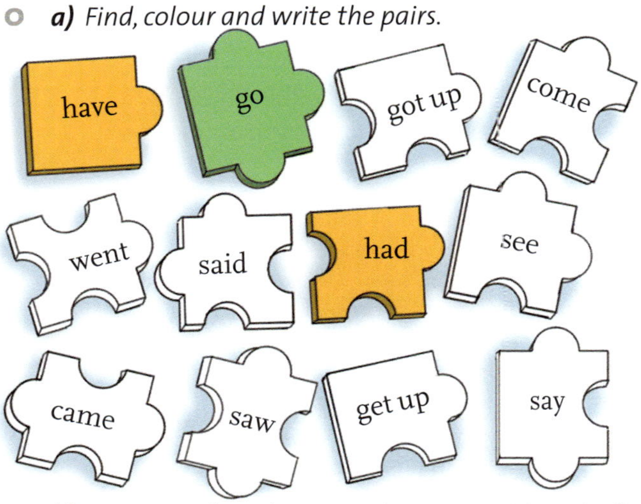

Infinitive:	Simple past:
have	*had*
go	

b) *Now complete the story about Tim with verbs from a).*

Last Saturday Tim ____________ early and ________ a big breakfast. Then he ________ to the park. Becky ____________, 'Mum isn't here. Lunch is at twelve. Don't be late!' Tim's friends ____________ to the park with their skateboards. They all ________ a really good time. Suddenly Tim ____________, 'Oh, no! It's one o'clock. I'm late!' At home Becky ____________, 'Sorry, Tim. You're too late for lunch, and I'm going now. But there's some food in the fridge.' Tim ____________ to the fridge. Sandwiches? Chicken? Potato salad? But oh, no! Just cold chips!

● **Now you**

6210
6211

Write five or more sentences about your last weekend in your exercise book.
You can use ideas from exercises 9 and 10.
On Saturday I ... In the afternoon ... On Sunday we ...

11 REVISION He doesn't do that (Simple present: negative statements)

► p. 88 • GF 7c (p. 137)

Complete the sentences about Barnabas.

Tim: Barnabas is a very good pet. He doesn't sleep (sleep) all day and he ________ (eat) too much. He ________ (take) fish from the fridge and he ________ (make) a mess.

12 Extra They didn't do that … (Simple past: negative statements)

► p. 89 • GF 19 (p. 146)

Write what Tim's grandparents didn't do 60 years ago. Complete the sentences.

call • listen • play • watch • wear • write

1 They didn't wear jeans. They ________ computer games.

2 They ________ to rap music. They ________ people on mobile phones.

6312 3 They ________ DVDs. They ________ e-mails.

Extra Now you

Write what you/your family didn't do yesterday. Write four funny sentences.

My grandma didn't climb a tree yesterday. My dad didn't play hockey.

____

____

____

____

Just for fun

Teacher: Jimmy, how do you spell 'Geography'?
Jimmy: G-e-o-g-r-a-f-y.
Teacher: The dictionary spells it with 'ph'.
Jimmy: You didn't ask me how the dictionary spells it.

13 Extra The Spring Show was great! (Simple past: mixed forms) ▸ p. 89 • GF 17–19 (pp. 144–146)

Complete the sentences with simple past forms.

1 The Spring Show __was__ (be) two days ago.

2 After the show Dan ________ (say), 'The pirate ship ________ (look) great.'

3 But Jo ________ (~~like~~) the pirate ship.

4 Sophie's Dance Club ________ (~~dance~~) till the end.

5 Poor Prunella. She ________ (~~see~~) the show.

6 The Spring Show ________ (~~be~~) just good. It ________ (be) fantastic!

14 Extra Questions and answers (Simple past) ▸ p. 89 • GF 20 (p. 146)

Match the questions and answers.
Then write the correct blue letter: t _ _ _ _ _ _. *What's the new word?*

1 Was the pirate scene good?	Yes, they were.	i
2 Were all the kids nervous?	No, they didn't.	k
3 Did Sophie dance in the show?	No, she wasn't.	e
4 Did Jack and Ananda sing?	No, he didn't.	t
5 Was Prunella at the show?	Yes, she did.	c
6 Did Jo play in the band?	Yes, it was. ▸	t

15 WORDS What's wrong? ▸ p. 89

Write correct words and find the word in the blue boxes.

1 tcyi

5 gzeanmia

6 rta

3 etncoi robda

4 gcxneiti

2 nsneeitrtig

1 Bristol is a very nice ... ▸ □□□□

2 Museums aren't boring. They're ... ▸ □□□□□□□□□□□

3 What clubs are there? – Look at the school ...! ▸ □□□□□□ □□□□□

4 This pirate story is really ... ▸ □□□□□□□□

5 Ananda writes for the school ... ▸ □□□□□□□□

6 Dan can paint. He likes ... ▸ □□□

6415 Let's go to the □□□□□□ !

16 STUDY SKILLS Unbekannte Wörter verstehen ▸ p. 96 · SF 6 (p. 124)

a) *Markiere die unbekannten Wörter gelb.*

Becky On my birthday Mum and Dad want to go with us to London to see a musical.
Tim Oh, no! That sounds boring!
Becky It's my birthday and I want to see The Phantom of the Opera.
This is what it says in my magazine.

> The Phantom of the Opera by Andrew Lloyd Webber is a tragic love story. The scene is Paris, in the year 1911. The phantom – a mysterious musical genius with a wonderful voice – wears a mask because his face is ugly. He lives under the Opera House, under the streets of Paris where people can't see him. Christine, a beautiful young opera singer, is taking lessons from a mysterious new teacher – the Phantom. He loves Christine, but she doesn't love him.

Tim Romantic stuff! Girls! That isn't for me.
Becky Tim, be quiet and listen!

> He wants to make her into the next big star of the Opera. Christine is afraid of the Phantom because he is a very strict teacher. Bad things happen at the Opera House. Suddenly somebody is dead. One day, Christine pulls the mask from the Phantom's face and ...

Tim Wow! Is he a real person or is he a ghost?
Is he really ugly and scary without his mask?
Cool! Let's go to see The Phantom of the Opera!

No, no! No phantoms! What about Clever cats? Yes, Clever cats!

b) *Wie kannst du diese Wörter erschließen? Manchmal treffen zwei Kästchen zu. Setze Häkchen (✓):*

	Bild	ähnliches deutsches Wort	Zusammenhang
phantom	☐	☑	☐
mask	☐	☐	☐
strict	☐	☐	☐
ugly	☐	☐	☐

c) *Schreib drei Wörter auf, die du durch die Bilder erschließen kannst.*

ugly (hässlich), ______________________

d) *Schreib fünf Wörter auf, die im Deutschen ähnlich sind. Schreib auch das deutsche Wort auf.*

phantom (Phantom), opera (Oper) ______________________

____

____

e) *Welche Wörter kannst du aus dem Zusammenhang erschließen?*

strict (streng), ______________________

____

f) *Schau dir deine markierten Wörter noch einmal an. Kannst du jetzt alle Wörter verstehen?*

17 WORKING WITH THE TEXT A pirate story ▸ pp. 96–98

a) *Look at pages 96–98 of your student's book again. Match the pictures and the titles A–D.*

A The cabin boy is scared
B Bonny finds out about the Silver Swordfish
C A happy ending for the real Jonah
D The pirates' terrible work

1 ☐

2 ☐

3 ☐

4 ☐

b) *What's wrong? Mark the wrong sentences and correct them.*

1 It was a dark and windy evening. The ships were in the harbour. Only two sailors from the Silver Swordfish were in the tavern.

Only two sailors ______________________________ .

2 Bonny and Captain Rackham climbed onto the Silver Swordfish. They had pistols and swords. They wanted to help the sailors on the ship.

They wanted ______________________________ .

3 The cabin boy cleaned the Captain's cabin. Then he was tired, so he was soon asleep. Suddenly Bonny saw him and said, 'Good luck for you, boy!'

Bonny said, ______________________________ !'

4 Jonah was cold and scared. He opened his eyes. He was still on the floor of the cabin.

He was ______________________________ .

● ***c)*** *Now you are Jo. Tell Dan about your dream in the simple past. Use the notes or your own ideas.*

1 I/be/cabin boy/pirate ship • 2 First/Captain and Bonny/kill/two sailors/on the Silver Swordfish • 3 In cabin/I see/that/Bonny/be/woman • 4 After that/pirates/want to/kill me • 5 I/be/on the plank!

I was a cabin boy on a pirate ship.

____

____

____

6617
6618

1 Fill in: *was* (2x), *were*, *wasn't*, *weren't*

There ______________ a pet show in Bristol last week.

There ______________ some beautiful cats – but they ______________ very clever. One cat ______________ beautiful – but he ______________ very clever ... Look!

2 Yesterday

Complete the sentences with verbs in the simple past.

1 Sophie ______________ her bike.

2 Toby ______________ to his judo lesson.

3 Jo ______________ after ten o'clock.

4 Tim and Florian ______________ a chocolate cake.

5 Dilip ______________ the guitar.

6 Becky and Lucy ______________ their friends.

1

clean

2
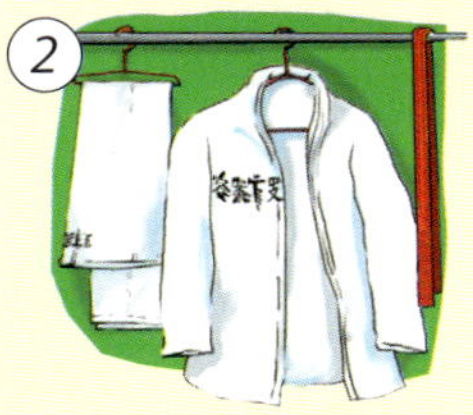
go

3

get up

4

make

5

practise

6

call

3 Clubs and activities

Where can you do these things? Complete the sentences.

1 You can act in plays in the ______________.

2 You can paint pictures in the ______________.

3 You can sing songs in the ______________.

4 You can do jazz dance in the ______________.

5 You can play the clarinet in the ______________.

16 points

● Now you

Write an e-mail to a friend about what you did last weekend in your exercise book. Use the simple past.
Ideas: do sport, see friends, have visitors, go to the park/the shops, watch TV/DVDs ...

6704
6705

Dear ...

I had a great weekend. On Friday I ...

Unit 6 Great places for kids

1 WORDS Places to go ▸ pp. 100–101

a) Write correct words.

a l i l v e g *village*	i t a n o s t ______
e m u s m u ______	r p k a ______
r e g b d i ______	o e t r w ______
h h r c u c ______	y t i c ______
r g d n a e ______	

b) Where did Florian and his cousin Leo go? Read the text and fill in the missing words from a).

I live in Bristol. It's a very old ______. My cousin Leo lives in a little ______ near Bath.

He lives with his mum and dad in a nice house with a ______.

Yesterday I went to his house on the train. He came to the ______ to meet me.

First, we went to the ______. It was great. We saw lots of interesting things, like old cars and funny bikes. Near the museum there was an old ______. It had a ______ with a clock.

After that we went to the ______. We walked over a little ______ and watched the fish in the water. Then we played football – and soon our football was in the water too ...

6800
6801

2 WORDS Word bridges

▸ p. 103

How many words can you make from the word bridges? Use the Dictionary in your student's book.

c ⌒ e *cage, cake,* ______________________________

____

h ⌒ e *horse,* ______________________________

e ⌒ e *eye,* ______________________________

3 REVISION I went there yesterday (Simple past: positive statements)

▸ p. 103 • GF 18 (p. 145)

Yesterday it was Saturday. Write what the kids did. Complete with the verb in the simple past.

Lucy Yesterday I *went* (go) to the library .

Then I ________ (practice) the guitar. I'm not very good, but it's fun.

Florian Well, I ________ (watch) sport on TV. It ________ (be) great.

Becky A friend ________ (come) after lunch and we ________ (go) shopping.

Tim Boring! I ________ (play) football with our team yesterday.

6903 After the game we ________ (have) an ice cream. Well I had three …

4 Extra No, you didn't, Prunella! (Simple past: negative statements)

▸ p. 103 • GF 19 (p. 146)

What does Sophie say? Write her sentences.

Prunella When I was a real girl 200 years ago, I went to school on my bike.

Sophie Prunella, you *didn't go to school on your bike.*

Prunella:	**Sophie:**
1 I watched TV every evening.	Oh, no. You didn't ________ .
2 I had an MP3 player.	That's silly. You ________ .
3 I played computer games.	No! ________ .
4 I collected phone cards.	Prunella, ________ .
5 I went to judo lessons.	And ________ .

5 Sophie likes the library because ... (Word order in subordinate clauses) ► p. 103 • GF 21 (p. 147)

a) *Match and write correct sentences with* ***because*** *or* ***when****.*

Sophie likes the library Dan hates it Prunella doesn't get up late Ananda doesn't like it	because when	*it's really quiet.* Jo sings the pirate song. she doesn't sleep. people argue.

1 *Sophie likes the library because it's really quiet.*

2 ______

3 ______

4 ______

Just for fun

What do you say when you meet a monster[1] with two heads?[2]

b) *Now write sentences about Barnabas with the words in the correct order.*

1 Barnabas is always happy when ... (him/Tim/feeds).

Barnabas ______.

2 Tim hates it when ... (on his face/Barnabas/sits).

______

3 The neighbour throws water at Barnabas because ... (in his garden/cats/he/doesn't like).

______

7005 ______

Now you

Complete the sentences.

My mum isn't happy when ______.

My teacher doesn't like it when ______.

6 PRONUNCIATION *th*: [θ] and [ð] ► p. 103 7

Listen to the words. Which th-sound is different? Colour it ***red****.*

1 there these thanks

2 other thousand bathroom

3 that thing those

7006 4 mouth both brother

5 another month father

6 with both bath

7 birthday throw then

Just for fun

Can you say this?

My mother thinks that there are a thousand things to do this Thursday.

[1] monster ('mɒnstə) [2] Hello, hello.

7 WORDS Good and bad words

▸ p. 103

a) *Which are good words? Write them in green. Which are bad words? Write them in red.*

be afraid • bad • beautiful • boring • dead • difficult • easy • fun • great • happy • interesting • poor • pretty • smile • scary • terrible

be afraid, bad, beautiful, ______________________

____

____

b) *Add more good and bad words in your exercise book.*

8 These aren't my things (this, that, these, those)

▸ p. 103

The twins' things are all in the wrong places. What does Jo say about his things? Use ***this, that, these, those.***

1 This ______ isn't my sweatshirt. That ______ is my sweatshirt on Dan's bed.

2 ______ isn't my T-shirt. ______ is my T-shirt on Dan's chair.

3 ______ aren't my shoes. ______ are my shoes over there in the corner.

4 ______ isn't my skateboard. ______ is my skateboard on the floor.

5 ______ aren't my socks. ______ are my socks on Dan's bed.

7108 6 ______ aren't my comics. ______ are my comics on Dan's shelf.

9 REVISION *There, their* or *they're*

▸ p. 103

Jo Where are my football boots?

Dan ______ over ______.

Jo No, they aren't. Mike and Leo put ______ boots over ______.

Dan Mmm. Right. They can't be your boots. ______ clean[1].

[1] clean [kli:n] *sauber*

10 REVISION A scary story? (Simple present, adverbs)

▸ p. 104 • GF 7 (pp. 136–137), GF 10–11 (pp. 139–140)

Complete the sentences. Use the simple present.

Florian Do you know (you/know) any scary stories? I like (like) them a lot.

Tim Well, maybe we ______ (have got) a poltergeist in our house. Becky ______ (often/hear) loud noises at night and my mum ______ (say) somebody ______ (sometimes/make) a mess in the kitchen. She ______ (often/see) cake or cheese on the floor the next morning.

Florian Wow! A real poltergeist? Fantastic! What ______ (he/do)? Where ______ (he/go)? ______ (he/drop) plates?

Tim Well, he ______ (do) really bad things. He ______ (always/go) to the kitchen and ______ (eat). But poltergeists ______ (eat). Hmmm. You know what? I ______ (think) our poltergeist ______ (be) my dad!

11 REVISION A school trip (Present progressive)

▸ p. 104 • GF 15a–b (pp. 142–143)

Lucy is on a school trip. She writes to her family. Use these verbs in the present progressive: **have, sit, wear, swim, play, take, talk**

Hi, Mum and Dad

It's great here. Here's a photo of me with my classmates. You can see we are having fun.

Mark ______ in the pool.

Dave and Emma ______ cards.

Rob ______ with me – with the big ice cream. Kim and Ann ______ to the teachers. Mr Fox ______ sunglasses. He looks like Will Smith! You can't see Nina because she ______ the photo.

See you soon
Lucy

7211

Rhyme time

At the end of our road
There's a funny old house,
Its door is black and red.
In the funny old house
lives a funny old ghost[1],
Oh no! He's under my bed!

[1] ghost [gəʊst] *Gespenst, Geist*

12 What's different? (Simple present and present progressive)

▸ p. 104 • GF 22 (pp. 147–148)

Today is different. What do the students and teachers usually do? What are they doing today? Circle the correct verb form.

On Fridays at 10.50 Form 7PK usually (has / is having) Maths, but today the students (are playing / play) a game. Form 7BW usually (reads / is reading) texts in the French lesson, but today the students (sing / are singing) songs. They always (listen / are listening) to their teachers, but now they (make / are making) a terrible noise. The students never (eat / are eating) in class but now they (are eating / eat) ice cream. They (are having / have) lots of fun. And Mr Kingsley is happy. Why? Well, it's the last day of school before the holidays!

13 Who's who? (Simple present and present progressive)

▸ p. 104 • GF 22 (pp. 147–148)

a) *Read about the five friends. Write the verbs in the simple present or present progressive.*

Maria likes (like) hamburgers, but today she is eating (eat) sandwiches.

Sally ________ (~~read~~) many books. She ________ (usually/read) magazines or comics.

Liz ________ (wear) her new sunglasses today. She ________ (eat) a big ice cream.

Jane ________ (like) books. She ________ (read) a detective story now.

Sarah ________ (~~like~~) sweet things.

b) *Who's who? Write their names.*

Number 1 is Maria. Number 3 is ________. Number 5 is ________.

7313 Number 2 is ________. Number 4 is ________.

14 WORDS A puzzle ▸ p. 104

a) *Complete the sentences.*

1 It's fun to e x p l o r e new places.

2 Do you live in a town, a city or a v _ _ _ _ _ _ ?

3 *Jo:* Sophie, you g _ _ _ _ _ _ all the time.

4 The library is usually quiet. We have to w _ _ _ _ _ _ !

5 The opposite of 'start' is ' _ _ _ _ _ h '.

b) *Write a new word with the letters in the blue boxes in a). The word is:* _ _ _ _ e .

15 REVISION Getting by in English ▸ p. 104

Your neighbours have got visitors, a boy and a girl from England.
You meet the English girl, Jenny, on the street. She doesn't understand German.
Ask her questions in English.

Frag sie ...

..., wie sie heißt. What's your name?

..., woher sie kommt. ______

..., wie alt sie ist. ______

..., ob sie Sport mag. ______

..., ob ihr Bruder Sport mag. ______

..., ob sie ein Haustier hat. ______

..., ob sie ein Fahrrad hat. ______

..., ob sie Gitarre spielt. ______

..., wer ihre Lieblingsband ist. ______

..., ob sie ein Handy hat. ______

7415 ..., wie ihre Telefonnummer ist. ______

16 Extra Just for fun ▸ p. 111

Read the jokes.

(1) Here are my favourite jokes:
A Hi! Are you coming to my party?
B No, I'm not. I'm going to see *Harry Potter*.
A Well, you can bring him too!

(2)
A: What date is it?
B: I don't know. Look at that newspaper on the chair.
A: But that's yesterday's newspaper ...

(3) I know some good jokes too:
What do elephants do in their free time?
– They watch elevision!

(4)
Teacher Say a sentence with 'I'.
Jimmy I is ...
Teacher No, no, Jimmy. That's wrong. You must say 'I am ...'
Jimmy OK. I am the ninth letter of the alphabet.

(5) Now it's my turn:
A I've got an invitation to Mike's party, but I can't go.
B Why not?
A Well, it says from 5 to 9 – and I'm 11.

(6) And here's another:
How do you know that carrots are good for your eyes?
– Because rabbits don't wear glasses.

(7) Here's my first joke:
What has got forty feet and sings?
– A school choir.

(8) My next joke is better:
A: Our dog is very brave[1]. He brings the newspaper for us every morning.
B: Why is that brave?
A: Because it's the neighbours' newspaper.

(9) And now here's the best joke!
What do cats eat on a hot day?
– Mice cream! Ha-ha-ha!

Now you

Which jokes are funny or silly? Which is your favourite? Which jokes don't you like? Write in your exercise book.

My favourite joke is number ... because ... *I don't like Lucy's first joke because ...*

[1] brave [breɪv] *tapfer, mutig*

1 Places: write the names.

1 ______________________ *3* ______________________

2 ______________________ *4* ______________________

2 What's right? Write correct sentences.

1 Presentations are fun ... (because/can/you/in groups/work).

____

2 The kids saw some great things ... (when/to the museum/they/went).

____

3 Sophie grumbled ... (because/used/too much glue/Jo/for the poster).

____

4 Ananda hates it ... (when/argue/people/all the time).

____

3 Complete with *this*, *that*, *these* and *those*.

Dan: No, it's wrong. ______________ is your cola and ______________ are your chips. ______________ orange juice is for me, and ______________ are my sandwiches.

4 Circle the correct verb form.

Lucy I (usually go / 'm usually going) to my guitar lesson on Tuesdays. But this week I (go / 'm going) on Wednesday. What about you?

Tim Well, we (don't have / aren't having) Maths homework on Wednesdays, but I (do / 'm doing) my Maths homework today because it was for yesterday.

16 points

Now you

7605
7606

Write about your city, town or village. What is there in your town? Ideas: houses, flats, shops, churches, museums, libraries, schools, parks, sports clubs. Write in your exercise book.
You can use these words: ***I live in ... It's a nice ... My favourite place is ... There are lots of ... We've got ...***

Jetzt kann ich ...

	Sehr gut!	OK	Verbessern!
HÖREN: Ich kann ...			
... Arbeitsanweisungen und Fragen im Unterricht verstehen.	☐	☐	☐
... Fragen über meine Freizeit, Schulklubs und meine Stadt verstehen.	☐	☐	☐
... die Auflösung der SHoCK-Team-Geschichte in Unit 6 verstehen.	☐	☐	☐
SPRECHEN: Ich kann ...			
... verschiedene Lebensmittel und Getränke nennen.	☐	☐	☐
... mit ***I'd like*** sagen, was ich haben möchte.	☐	☐	☐
... mit dem *present progressive* sagen, was jemand gerade tut oder was gerade geschieht.	☐	☐	☐
... mit dem *simple past* sagen, was in der Vergangenheit war oder geschah.	☐	☐	☐
... die Wörter der Units 4–6 richtig aussprechen.	☐	☐	☐
... die Geschichte vom SHoCK-Team in groben Zügen nacherzählen.	☐	☐	☐
LESEN: Ich kann ...			
... die Arbeitsanweisungen in meinem Buch/Workbook verstehen.	☐	☐	☐
... Geschichten und Gedichte der Units 4–6 lesen und verstehen.	☐	☐	☐
SCHREIBEN: Ich kann ...			
... eine Einkaufsliste für Lebensmittel und Getränke schreiben.	☐	☐	☐
... einen kleinen Text über meine Stadt schreiben.	☐	☐	☐
... eine kurze E-Mail schreiben.	☐	☐	☐
... eine Einladung zu einer Party oder einem Grillfest schreiben.	☐	☐	☐
... *some* und *any* richtig benutzen.	☐	☐	☐
LAND UND LEUTE: Ich weiß ...			
..., was es für Klubs und Aktivitäten in britischen Schulen gibt.	☐	☐	☐
..., wie sich der britische Schulalltag vom deutschen unterscheidet.	☐	☐	☐
LERNEN UND ARBEITEN: Ich kann ...			
... Vokabeln auf verschiedene Weise lernen.	☐	☐	☐
... einfache Notizen nach *key words* anfertigen.	☐	☐	☐
... auf verschiedene Weise unbekannte Wörter erschließen.	☐	☐	☐
... mit drei anderen zusammen eine *placemat activity* bearbeiten.	☐	☐	☐

WIE ICH MICH VERBESSERN KÖNNTE: Ich könnte ...

- ... häufiger im Dictionary nachschlagen. ☐
- ... häufiger im Skills File lesen. ☐
- ... häufiger im Grammar File nachschauen. ☐
- ... nützliche Sätze für bestimmte Situationen auswendig lernen. ☐
- ... kurze Texte aus meinem Buch abschreiben. ☐
- ... mit einem Partner oder zu dritt Rollenspiele einüben. ☐
- ... eine/n englische/n E-Freund/in suchen. ☐

- Hier kannst du deine Antworten im Checkpoint überprüfen. Falls du Probleme mit den jeweiligen Aufgaben hattest, folge den Lernhilfen in der rechten Spalte. Die Verweise beziehen sich auf dein Schülerbuch oder dein Workbook.
- Deine Punktzahl kannst du ermitteln, indem du dir für jede richtige Lösung einen Punkt gibst. Schreib deine Gesamtpunktzahl in das gelbe Kästchen unten links.

1 What can you see in the classroom?

1 window *5* teacher

2 board *6* table

3 timetable *7* apple

8 P. *4* calendar *8* chair

- Schau dir Skills File 1 zu „Wörter lernen" (S. 122–123) noch einmal an.
- Lern die Wörter mithilfe des Vocabulary (S. 156–160).

2 Complete.

1 Barnabas isn't a parrot.

He 's a cat.

2 'I 'm a very nice pet.

I 'm not a mad cat!'

3 They aren't classmates.

6 P. They 're brother and sister.

- Die Formen von *be* kannst du dir im Grammar File 2a (S. 132) noch einmal ansehen.
- Löse die Aufgaben 4–5 im Practice-Teil (S. 26), um die Formen von *be* sicher zu verwenden.

3 Write what they *have got* and what they *haven't got*.

1 The Hansons have got a B&B. It has got five rooms.

2 The Kapoors haven't got a house. They have got a flat and a shop.

6 P. *3* Ananda has got a brother, but she hasn't got a pet.

- Lern die Formen von *have got* mithilfe des Grammar File 5a (S. 134).
- Wiederhole die Übungen 13–14a zu *have got* im Practice-Teil (S. 29–30).

Now you (Musterlösung)

Hi!
I'm your new friend from Germany. My name is Heike and I'm from Kassel. I'm 11 years old. I've got a brother, Markus. He's 13. My favourite sport is basketball. I can play badminton too. My favourite subjects are Maths and Music. I've got a dog, Benno. Have you got a pet?
Bye!

- Falls du Schwierigkeiten hattest, einen zusammenhängenden Text zu schreiben, schau dir in deinem Workbook die Aufgabe 22 (S. 20) noch einmal an und schreib deinen Text zu Aufgabe 22 noch einmal in dein Heft.
- Lern die Formen von *be* (Grammar File 2a, S. 132), *can* (Grammar File 3a, S. 133) und *have got* (Grammar File 5a, S. 134).

Ich habe ______ Punkte von 20.

20–17: Sehr gut. Weiter so!
16–13: Schon recht gut.
Unter 13: Genauer lernen!

1 What are they? Label the pets.

1 *budgie* 4 *tortoise*

2 *rabbit* 5 *guinea pig*

6 P. 3 *mouse* 6 *horse*

Falls du Probleme hattest:

- Schau dir Skills File 1 zu „Wörter lernen" (S. 122–123) noch einmal an.
- Lern die Vokabeln noch einmal (S. 161–162).

2 *'s* or *s'* ?

1 The (Kapoors) *Kapoors'* flat is over the shop.

2 7PK is (Mr Kingsley) *Mr Kingsley's* form.

3 Bill and Ben are (Dan and Jo) *Dan and Jo's* pets.

4 P. 4 Barnabas is (Tim) *Tim's* cat.

- Wie du *'s* und *s'* richtig benutzt, kannst du im Grammar File 9 (S. 138) nachlesen.
- Löse die Aufgabe 16 im Practice-Teil (S. 47) noch einmal, um den *s*-Genitiv zu üben.

3 *His*, *her*, *its* or *their*?

1 The Carter-Browns and all *their* pets are at home today.

2 Prunella is at home. Sophie's room is *her* room too.

3 Jack is in the park with *his* dad.

4 P. 4 Sophie's cousin Emma has got a tortoise. What's *its* name?

- Die Possessivbegleiter findest du im Grammar File 8 (S. 138).
- Wiederhole die Übung 15 im Practice-Teil (S. 46), um die Possessivbegleiter sicher zu benutzen.

4 Complete the sentences with: *like*, *likes* (✓), *doesn't like*, *don't like* (✗)

1 Lucy *likes* horses and fish. She *doesn't like* cats.

2 Jo and Tim *don't like* fish, but they *like* horses and cats.

3 Florian *doesn't like* fish or cats.

6 P. 4 Becky *likes* all the pets.

- Schau dir Grammar File 7a und 7c (S. 136–137) an, um die positiven und negativen Formen im *simple present* zu lernen.
- Löse die Aufgaben 3 (S. 42), 6a (S. 43) und 10–11a (S. 45) im Practice-Teil.

Now you (Musterlösung)

I've got a hamster. His name is Nick He's brown and white. He eats hamster food and carrots. He lives in a nice cage in the living room. My friend has got a cat. Her name is Pam. She's black and white. She eats cat food and fish. I like dogs, cats, horses and hamsters. I don't like fish or budgies.

- Falls du Schwierigkeiten hattest, einen zusammenhängenden Text zu schreiben, lies dir Skills File 3 zu Mindmaps (S. 125) durch. Dort erfährst du, wie du deine Ideen für einen Text sammeln und ordnen kannst.
- Die Formen von *have got* findest du im Grammar File 5a (S. 134).
- *Simple present*-Formen kannst du im Grammar File 7a/c (S. 136–137) nachschlagen.

Ich habe ______ Punkte von 20.

20–17: Sehr gut. Weiter so!
16–13: Schon recht gut.
Unter 13: Genauer lernen!

1 Sports and hobbies

1 Jack *makes models*.

2 Sophie *goes riding*.

3 Dilip *plays the guitar*.

4 P. 4 Ananda *collects stamps*.

2 Ask about the people in ( ).

1 *Do Dan and Sophie like music?*

2 *Does Sophie play tennis?*

3 *Do you write e-mails?*

4 P. 4 *Does Jack's dad do yoga?*

3 Make correct sentences.

1 *Jay never goes to football matches.*

2 *I don't often write e-mails.*

3 *Does Becky play basketball?*

4 P. 4 *Where does Prunella play tennis?*

4 Write what they *have to* do or *don't have to* do.

1 At school we *have to* listen to the teacher.

2 Most days Jack *has to* help at the B&B.

3 In the holidays we *don't have to* get up early.

4 P. 4 Prunella *doesn't have to* go to school.

Now you (Musterlösung)

I like sport. I play football at school and I do judo on Tuesdays. I collect posters for my room too. My friend plays basketball and he makes models. My dad plays tennis and my mum plays the piano. My sister goes riding and she collects DVDs.

Ich habe ______ Punkte von 16.

16–14: Sehr gut. Weiter so!
13–11: Schon recht gut.
Unter 11: Genauer lernen!

Falls du Probleme hattest:

- Schau dir Skills File 1 zu „Wörter lernen" (S. 122–123) noch einmal an.
- Lern die Wörter mithilfe des Vocabulary (S. 166–167).
- Löse die Aufgaben 1–2 im Practice-Teil (S. 58).

- Wie du Fragen im *simple present* richtig bildest, erfährst du im Grammar File 10a (S. 139).
- Wiederhole die Übungen 4–7 im Practice-Teil (S. 59).

- Lies Grammar File 10–11 (S. 139–140).
- Mach die Übungen 10 (S. 61) und 15a (S. 63) im Practice-Teil noch einmal.

- Schau dir Grammar File 12 zu *have to* (S. 141) an.
- Übe die Formen von *have to* mithilfe der Aufgabe 17 im Practice-Teil (S. 63).

- Falls du Schwierigkeiten hattest, einen Text zu schreiben, lies dir Skills File 3 zu Mindmaps (S. 125) noch einmal durch.
- Grammar File 7 (S. 136–137) verdeutlicht dir noch einmal den Gebrauch des *simple present*.

1 What does Mrs Carter-Brown need from the shops?

1 *cheese*
2 *lemonade*
3 *chicken*
4 *orange juice*
5 *sausages*
6 *ice cream*

6 P.

Falls du Probleme hattest:

- Schau dir Skills File 1 zu „Wörter lernen" (S. 122–123) noch einmal an.
- Lern die Vokabeln (S. 170–171).

2 Complete with: *me*, *him*, *her*, *it*, *them*

1 *Tim* Where's Mum's shopping list? I can't find *it*.
2 *Becky* I don't know. Don't ask *me*.
3 *Tim* Well, where's Mum? Let's ask *her*.
4 *Becky* Where are Mum and Dad? I can't see *them*.
5 *Tim* Dad is in the garden. Let's ask *him*.

5 P.

- Die Objektformen der Personalpronomen findest du im Grammar File 13 (S. 141).
- Üben kannst du sie mithilfe der Aufgaben 3 und 4 im Practice-Teil (S. 75–76).

3 What's in the fridge? *Some* or *any*?

1 *Tim* There's *some* fruit, but there aren't *any* carrots.
2 *Becky* And is there *any* milk?
3 *Tim* No, but there's *some* lemonade.

4 P.

- Wie du *some* und *any* richtig verwendest, zeigt dir Grammar File 14 (S. 142).
- Löse die Aufgabe 7a im Practice-Teil (S. 77).

4 What*'s happening* at the station?

1 A man *is reading* a newspaper.
2 Two girls *are getting on* the train.
3 A boy *is calling* somebody on his mobile.
4 A woman *is giving* a girl some money.
5 Two boys *are running* to the train.

5 P.

- Im Grammar File 15a/b (S. 142–143) kannst du nachlesen, wann du das *present progressive* benutzt und wie du die Formen bildest.
- Wiederhole die Aufgaben 9–10 im Practice-Teil (S. 78).

Now you (Musterlösung)

I'm having a big barbecue for my birthday. All my friends and classmates are here. They're giving me presents. There's great food. We're eating chicken, sausages and potato salad. My friends are singing 'Happy birthday to you'. Now we're dancing. The music is fantastic. We're having a great time.

Ich habe ☐ Punkte von 20.

20–17: Sehr gut. Weiter so!
16–13: Schon recht gut.
Unter 13: Genauer lernen!

- Falls du Schwierigkeiten hattest, einen Text zu schreiben, schau dir die Aufgaben 13 (S. 54) und 18 (S. 56) in deinem Workbook noch einmal an und schreib den Text von 18a ab.
- Im Grammar File 7 (S. 136–137) findest du Informationen zum *simple present* und Grammar File 15 (S. 142–143) zeigt dir den Gebrauch des *present progressive*.

1 Fill in: *was* (2x), *were*, *wasn't*, *weren't*

There *was* a pet show in Bristol last week.

There *were* some beautiful cats – but they *weren't* very clever.

One cat *wasn't* beautiful – but he *was* very clever ... Look!

5 P.

2 Yesterday

1 Sophie *cleaned* her bike.

2 Toby *went* to his judo lesson.

3 Jo *got up* after ten o'clock.

4 Tim and Florian *made* a chocolate cake.

5 Dilip *practised* the guitar.

6 Becky and Lucy *called* their friends.

6 P.

3 Clubs and activities

1 You can act in plays in the *Drama Club*.

2 You can paint pictures in the *Art Club*.

3 You can sing songs in the *Junior Choir*.

4 You can do jazz dance in the *Dance Club*.

5 You can play the clarinet in the *Junior Band*.

5 P.

Now you (Musterlösung)

Dear ...
I had a great weekend. On Friday I went swimming with my friends. On Saturday we went to the shops and we had sausages and chips for lunch.
In the evening I watched a funny film on TV.
On Sunday I got up very late. My aunt and uncle came for lunch. After lunch we went to the park with our dog. Great!
School tomorrow – not so great.
Love ...

Ich habe ______ Punkte von 16.

16–14: Sehr gut. Weiter so!
13–11: Schon recht gut.
Unter 11: Genauer lernen!

Falls du Probleme hattest:

- Die *simple past*-Formen von *be* findest du im Grammar File 17 (S. 144).
- Die Aufgabe 3 im Practice-Teil (S. 90) bietet dir eine Übungsmöglichkeit dieser Formen.

- Schlag Grammar File 18 (S. 145) auf, um zu sehen, wie die regelmäßigen Formen im *simple past* gebildet werden und wie die unregelmäßigen Formen aussehen.
- Eine Liste von unregelmäßigen Verben findest du auf der S. 178 unten. Dort kannst du nachschauen, wenn dir eine Form nicht einfällt.
- Löse die Aufgaben 6 (S. 91) und 9 (S. 92) im Practice-Teil, um den Gebrauch des *simple past* besser zu beherrschen.

- Falls du vergessen hast, wie man die Namen der Klubs schreibt, dann schau dir in deinem Schülerbuch die S. 84–85 an.
- Such dort die Namen der Klubs und schreib sie in dein Heft.

- Falls du Schwierigkeiten hattest, deine Gedanken zu ordnen, schau dir Skills File 3 zu Mindmaps (S. 125) noch einmal an.
- Im Grammar File 18 (S. 145) findest du die Bildung von regelmäßigen Formen im *simple past*.
- Die unregelmäßigen Verben stehen auf der S. 178 unten.

1 Places: write the names.

1 church 3 library

4 P. 2 bridge 4 tower

2 What's right? Write correct sentences.

1 Presentations are fun ...
... because you can work in groups.

2 The kids saw some great things ...
... when they went to the museum.

3 Sophie grumbled ...
... because Jo used too much glue for the poster.

4 Ananda hates it ...
4 P. ... when people argue all the time.

3 Complete with *this*, *that*, *these* and *those*.

Dan: No, it's wrong. This is your cola and these are your chips. That orange juice is for me, and

4 P. those are my sandwiches.

4 Circle the correct verb form.

Lucy I (usually go / 'm usually going) to my guitar lesson on Tuesdays. But this week I (go / 'm going) on Wednesday. What about you?

Tim Well, we (don't have / aren't having) Maths homework on Wednesdays, but I (do / 'm doing) my Maths homework

4 P. today because it was for yesterday.

Now you (Musterlösung)

I live in ... It's a nice town. There are lots of nice places for kids. In the town centre there are lots of shops. We've got a nice library too. It has got lots of books and DVDs. There's a nice cinema. My school is near the park. I often go to the park after school with my friends because we can play football there.

Ich habe ☐ Punkte von 16.

16–14: Sehr gut. Weiter so!
13–11: Schon recht gut.
Unter 11: Genauer lernen!

Falls du Probleme hattest:

- Lies Skills File 1 (S. 122–123).
- Lern die Wörter (S. 177).

- Schau dir die Wortstellung in Nebensätzen im Grammar File 21 (S. 147) an.
- Wiederhole die Übung 4 im Practice-Teil (S. 107).

- Lies den blauen Kasten im Vocabulary auf der S. 178 zu *this, that – these, those.*
- Löse die Aufgabe 6 im Practice-Teil (S. 107).

- Falls du nicht weißt, wann du die einfache Form der Gegenwart (*simple present*) und wann du die Verlaufsform (*present progressive*) verwenden musst, schau dir Grammar File 22 (S. 147–148) an.
- Übe den Gebrauch dieser beiden Formen mithilfe der Aufgaben 7 und 9 im Practice-Teil (S. 108).

- Falls du zu wenig über deine Stadt oder dein Dorf weißt, kannst du versuchen, im Internet Informationen zu sammeln.
- Eine Mindmap (Skills File 3, S. 125) kann dir beim Sammeln und Ordnen deiner Gedanken behilflich sein.
- Den Gebrauch des *simple present* kannst du im Grammar File 7 (S. 136–137) und Grammar File 22 (S. 147–148) nachschlagen.

Unit 1

GF 1 Personal pronouns ▸ *GF (p. 131)*

Jack is nice. ▸ He's nice.
My pencil is red. ▸ It's red.

Personalpronomen sind:
I, you, he, she, it, we, you, they.

You are nice. = Du bist nett. / Ihr seid nett. / Sie sind nett.

! Die deutschen Personalpronomen **du**, **ihr** und **Sie** heißen im Englischen alle ***you***.

Bei einer männlichen Person	– he	Bei einem Haustier	– he oder she
Bei einer weiblichen Person	– she	Bei einem Tier ohne Namen	– it
Bei einem Ding oder Begriff	– it	Bei mehreren Personen, Dingen, Tieren	– they

GF 2 The verb *(to) be* ▸ *GF (p. 132)*

a) Statements

Langformen: +	–	**Kurzformen:** +	–
I am	I am not	I'm	I'm not
you are	you are not	you're	you aren't
he/she/it is	he/she/it is not	he's/she's/it's	he/she/it isn't
we are	we are not	we're	we aren't
you are	you are not	you're	you aren't
they are	they are not	they're	they aren't

Beim Sprechen und in persönlichen Briefen werden meist die Kurzformen von *be* verwendet.

b) Questions

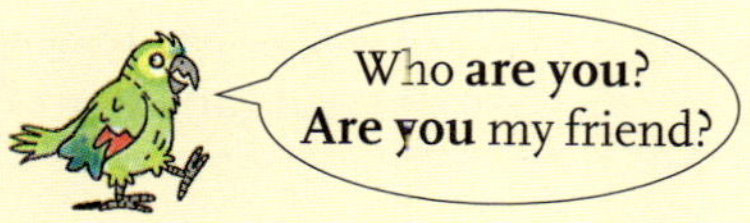

Fragen kannst du **mit Fragewort** *(Who …?)* oder **ohne Fragewort** *(Are you …?)* stellen.

Am I …? / Are you …? / Is he/she/it …?
Are we …? / Are you …? / Are they …?

Nach einem Fragewort wird *is* oft verkürzt:
Who's that? / Where's my book? / What's your name?

c) Short answers

+	–
Yes, I am.	No, I'm not.
Yes, you are.	No, you aren't.
Yes, he/she/it is.	No, he/she/it isn't.
Yes, we/you/they are.	No, we/you/they aren't.

! Nach *Yes* darfst du keine Kurzform verwenden.
Also nur
Yes, I am. / ***Yes, we are.***
usw.

GF 3 *can* ▸ *GF (p. 133)*

a) Statements

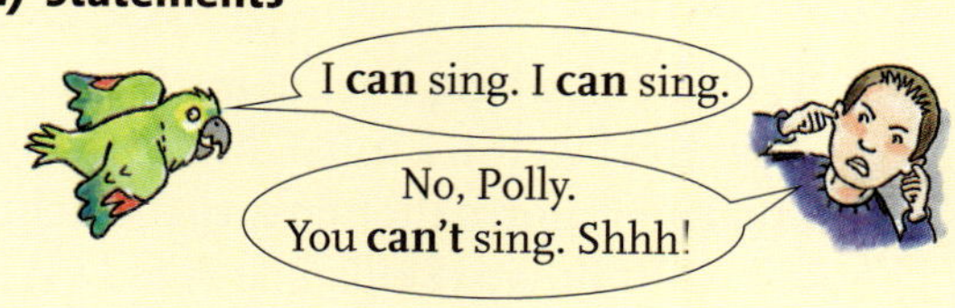

Mit *can* und *can't* drückst du aus, was jemand tun kann oder nicht tun kann.
Es heißt immer *can* bzw. *can't*, egal, ob es um *I, you, he* oder *we* usw. geht.

b) Questions and short answers

Can you do tricks? – **Yes, I** can. / **No, I** can't.

◂ So bildest du Fragen und Kurzantworten mit *can* und *can't*.

GF 4 Imperatives ▸ *GF (p. 134)*

Write the words on the board, please.

Polly, don't sing. And don't talk, please.

Im Englischen gibt es nur eine Befehlsform, egal, mit wem du sprichst.
Bei einem Verbot (= einem verneinten Befehl) steht *don't* davor:
Don't walk. (Langform: *Do not walk.*)

GF 5 The verb *have got* ▸ *GF (pp. 134–135)*

a) Statements

Jack has got a parrot.

Sophie hasn't got a parrot. She's got a dog.

Jo and Dan have got pets too.

Die Form *have got* steht bei *I, you, we* und *they*.
Bei *he/she/it* heißt die Form *has got*.

! – *She's got a dog.* = *She has got a dog.*
(nicht: *She ~~is~~ got a dog.*)
– *She's very nice.* = *She is very nice.*

Langformen: +	–	**Kurzformen:** +	–
I have got	I have not got	I've got	I haven't got
you have got	you have not got	you've got	you haven't got
he/she/it has got	he/she/it has not got	he's/she's/it's got	he/she/it hasn't got
we have got	we have not got	we've got	we haven't got
you have got	you have not got	you've got	you haven't got
they have got	they have not got	they've got	they haven't got

b) Questions

Have you got a pet? / Has Jack got a pet?

! In Fragen steht *got* nach dem Subjekt (*you, Jack*).

Have I/you got ...?	Has he/she/it got ...?	Have we/you got ...?	Have they got ...?

c) Short answers

Have you got a pet? – **Yes, I have. / No, I haven't.**
Has Jack got a pet? – **Yes, he has.**

! **1** Bei der Kurzantwort fällt das *got* weg.
2 Nach *Yes* musst du immer die Langform verwenden.

Unit 2

GF 6 The plural of nouns ▸ *GF (p. 135)*

a parrot
(Singular)

two parrots [s]
(Plural)

Du bildest den Plural (die Mehrzahl) eines Nomens, indem du ***s*** an das Nomen anhängst.

GF 7 The simple present ▸ *GF (pp. 136–137)*

a) Positive statements

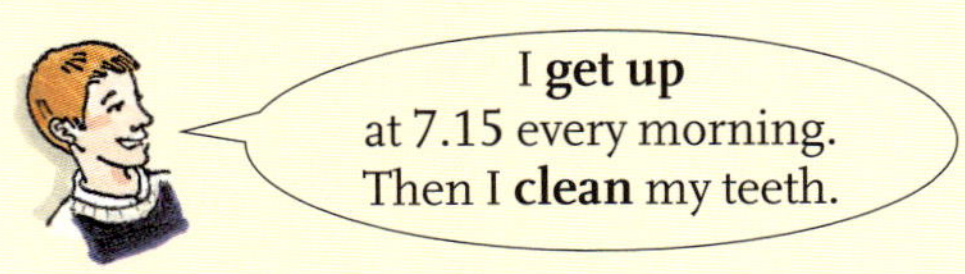

◂ Jo redet hier über das, was er regelmäßig tut (*every morning*, „jeden Morgen"). Die Sätze stehen im *simple present*.

I/You	like	apples and bananas.
He/She/It	likes	
We/You/They	like	

Simple present?
He, she, it?
YES, YES! An 's'!

He, she, it –
das „s" muss mit!

c) Negative statements

I	don't	like	apples and bananas.
You	don't	like	
He/She/It	doesn't	like	
We/You/They	don't	like	

Polly says,
In *doesn't* + verb
there's just one 's'!

GF 8 Possessive determiners ▸ GF (p. 138)

my	room	*mein Zimmer*	our	room	*unser Zimmer*
your	room	*dein/Ihr Zimmer*	your	room	*euer/Ihr Zimmer*
his	room	*sein Zimmer*	their	room	*ihr Zimmer*
her	room	*ihr Zimmer*			
its	room	*sein/ihr Zimmer*			

GF 9 The possessive form ▸ GF (p. 138)

Singular: Nomen + 's (the **dog's** basket)
Plural: Pluralform des Nomens + ' (the **rabbits'** hutch)

Wenn du sagen willst, dass jemandem etwas gehört, benutzt du den ***s*-Genitiv**.

! Anders als im Deutschen wird im Englischen das ***s*** mit einem Apostroph (**'**) angehängt.

Unit 3

GF 10 The simple present ▸ GF (pp. 139–140)

a) Yes/No questions

Do	I	like ...?	Do	we	like ...?
Do	you	like ...?	Do	you	like ...?
Does	he/she/it	like ...?	Do	they	like ...?

Polly says,
In questions with *Does*
there's just one 's'!

b) Short answers

Do you **get up** early? – **Yes, I** do. / **No, I** don't.
Does Jack **like** computer games? – **Yes, he** does.

Entscheidungsfragen werden nicht nur mit *Yes* oder *No* beantwortet, sondern mit einer Kurzantwort.

c) Questions with question words

When do you **play** tennis, Prunella?
And **where do** you **play**?

Do *you* ***play*** *tennis?*		(Entscheidungsfrage)
When ***do*** *you* ***play*** *tennis?*		(Fragen mit Fragewort: *When,*
How ***does*** *he* ***play*** *tennis?*		*Where, What, How, Why*)

GF 11 Adverbs of frequency: word order ▸ GF (p. 140)

I never **sleep**.
I usually **go** in all the rooms at night.

Jack always **writes** great stories.
Jack schreibt immer tolle Geschichten.

Prunella **can** often **help** Sophie.
Prunella kann Sophie oft helfen.

I'**m** usually nice to Sophie.

◂ Häufigkeitsadverbien (*always, usually, often, sometimes, never*) stehen gewöhnlich direkt **vor dem Vollverb** (z.B. *sleep, go*).

! Anders als im Deutschen stehen Häufigkeitsadverbien nie zwischen Verb und Objekt:

		Verb	Objekt			Verb		Objekt
Jo	*often*	***plays***	***football*** .		*Jo*	***spielt***	*oft*	***Fußball*** .

◂ Häufigkeitsadverbien stehen **hinter** *am/are/is*.

GF 12 The verb *(to) have to* ▸ GF (p. 141)

I **have to** get up early every day.
I **have to** help in the kitchen.

Wenn du ausdrücken willst, was du oder andere tun müssen, benutzt du *have to*.

+		–		?	
I/you	have to	I/you	don't have to	Do I/you	have to ...?
he/she/it	has to	he/she/it	doesn't have to	Does he/she/it	have to ...?
we/you/they	have to	we/you/they	don't have to	Do we/you/they	have to ...?

Unit 4

GF 13 Personal pronouns: object forms ▶ *GF (p. 141)*

I can't do this homework. You can help me.
You don't know me, but I know you.
There's Jack. **He**'s nice. Can you see him?

◀ Bei den Personalpronomen unterscheiden wir die **Subjektformen** *(I, you, he, ...)* und die **Objektformen** *(me, you, him, her, it, us, you, them)*.

I like her.	Ich mag **sie**.	*(Sophie, meine Lehrerin, ...)*
I like it.	Ich mag **sie**.	*(meine Schule, die Stadt, ...)*
I like them.	Ich mag **sie**.	*(meine Eltern, die Stiefel, ...)*

! Das deutsche „sie" (Objektform) kann auf Englisch *her, it* oder *them* heißen.

GF 14 *some* and *any* ▶ *GF (p. 142)*

We've got **some** crisps and **some** cheese.
Wir haben einige Kartoffelchips und etwas Käse.

◀ *some* steht vor allem in bejahten Aussagesätzen. Es kann „einige" oder „etwas" heißen.

But we haven't got **any** orange juice.
Have we got **any** biscuits?
Aber wir haben keinen Orangensaft. Haben wir Kekse?

◀ In verneinten Aussagesätzen und in Fragen steht meist *any*.

Angebot: Would you like **some** biscuits?
Bitte: Can I have **some** juice, please?

! Wenn du mit einer Frage etwas anbietest oder um etwas bittest, verwendest du *some*.

GF 15 The present progressive ▶ *GF (pp. 142–143)*

a) The simple present and the present progressive

simple present – I **help** in the kitchen **every day**.

present progressive – **I'm helping** in the kitchen **now**.

Mit dem ***simple present*** (einfache Form der Gegenwart) sprichst du über das, was jemand jeden Tag tut.

Wenn du allerdings sagen möchtest, dass jemand **gerade in diesem Moment** etwas tut, musst du das ***present progressive*** (Verlaufsform der Gegenwart) verwenden.

b) The present progressive: positive and negative statements

Sophie is helping in the kitchen.
Sophie hilft (gerade) in der Küche.

Du bildest das *present progressive* mit *am/are/is* + *-ing*-Form des Verbs: *Sophie **is helping**. Emily **isn't helping**.*

+		–	
I'm	working	I'm not	working
you're		you aren't	
he's/she's/it's		he isn't/she isn't/it isn't	
we're		we aren't	
you're		you aren't	
they're		they aren't	

c) The present progressive: questions and short answers

Are you working, Dad? – Yes, I am. / No, I'm not.
Is Sophie making a salad? – Yes, she is. / No, she isn't.

In Fragen sind Subjekt *(you, Sophie)* und *am/are/is* vertauscht. Die Kurzantworten sind genauso wie beim Verb *be*.

Unit 5

GF 16 The simple past ▶ *GF (p. 144)*

Last week Ananda followed Mr Green to the station.
Letzte Woche ist Ananda Mr. Green zum Bahnhof gefolgt.

Mit dem *simple past* kannst du über Vergangenes berichten. Mit Zeitangaben wie *last week, yesterday, three days ago* sagst du, **wann** etwas geschehen ist oder **wann** jemand etwas getan hat.

GF 17 The simple past of the verb *(to) be* ▸ GF (p. 144)

Jo: The dress rehearsal **was** great.
We **were** all good.

Dan: Jack **wasn't** bad. The girls **weren't** bad.
And you **were** fantastic, Jo!

Jo: Really? **Was** I fantastic?

Dan: Well ... **no, you weren't.** Not really.

Beim *simple past* von *be* gibt es nur zwei Formen:
I, he/she/it *was* ***you, we, they*** *were*

◂ Die verneinten Formen heißen ***wasn't*** und ***weren't***.

◂ Die Frage bildest du mit ***Was I ... / Were you ...?*** usw.

◂ Die Kurzantworten heißen ***Yes, I was. / No, you weren't.*** usw.

GF 18 The simple past: positive statements ▸ GF (p. 145)

a) Regular verbs

I **watched** Mr Green on Monday.
Ananda **followed** him yesterday.

Bei regelmäßigen Verben bildest du das *simple past* durch Anhängen von ***ed*** an den Infinitiv:
watch → watched, follow → followed, talk → talked.

b) Irregular verbs

Lots of people went to the Spring Show.
(Infinitiv: **go**)

Wie im Deutschen gibt es auch im Englischen eine Reihe unregelmäßiger Verben, deren *simple past*-Formen du einzeln lernen musst. ▸ *Unregelmäßige Verben (p. 178)*

GF 19 Extra The simple past: negative statements ▸ GF (p. 146)

I **didn't follow** Mr Green yesterday.
Ananda **didn't have** time.

Eine Aussage im *simple past* verneinst du immer mit ***didn't*** + **Infinitiv**.

GF 20 Extra The simple past: questions and short answers ▸ GF (p. 146)

Did your dad **go** to the Spring Show, Jo?
– **Yes, he** did. / **No, he** didn't.

Fragen im *simple past* bildest du immer mit ***did***:
Did he go? (Nicht: *Did he ~~went~~?*)

Unit 6

GF 21 Word order in subordinate clauses ▸ GF (p. 147)

I like the library **because I like books.** And I like the library **because it's quiet.**

Anders als im Deutschen ist die Wortstellung im Nebensatz genauso wie im Hauptsatz, nämlich **Subjekt – Verb (– Objekt)**:

Hauptsatz				Nebensatz		
S	**V**	**O**		**S**	**V**	**O**
I	*like*	*the library*	*because*	*I*	*like*	*books.*
		...,	*weil*	*ich*	*Bücher*	*mag.*

GF 22 The simple present and the present progressive in contrast ▸ GF (pp. 147–148)

Simple present:
- Die **einfache Form** der Gegenwart *(simple present)* drückt aus, dass jemand etwas **wiederholt** tut:
  Polly usually cleans her cage on Saturdays.
- Die **einfache Form** wird auch verwendet, um **aufeinanderfolgende Handlungen** zu beschreiben, z.B. wenn man eine Geschichte erzählt (oft mit *First ..., then ..., after that ...*):
  First Ananda follows Mr Green to the station, then she watches him.
  After that she calls Jack on her mobile.

Present progressive:
Die **Verlaufsform** der Gegenwart *(present progressive)* drückt aus, dass jemand **gerade im Moment** etwas tut. Die Handlung ist **noch nicht abgeschlossen**:
Look, Polly is cleaning her cage now.